A Heart for the Holidays

THE SPIRIT OF SIMPLE LIVING

A Heart *for the* Holidays

SHARON HANBY-ROBIE

Guideposts®
CARMEL, NEW YORK 10512

Acknowledgments

Every attempt has been made to credit the sources of copyrighted material used in this book. If any such acknowledgment has been inadvertently omitted or miscredited, receipt of such information would be appreciated.

All material that originally appeared in *Daily Guideposts* is reprinted with permission.

Scripture quotations marked (KJV) are taken from *The King James Version of the Bible.*

Scripture quotations marked (MSG) are taken from *The Message.* Copyright © 1993, 1994, 1995, 1996, 2000, 2001, 2002 by Eugene H. Peterson.

Scripture quotations marked (NAS) are taken from the *New American Standard Bible,* Copyright © The Lockman Foundation, 1960, 1962, 1963, 1968, 1971, 1972, 1973, 1975, 1977. Used by permission.

Scripture quotations marked (NIV) are taken from *The Holy Bible, New International Version.* Copyright © 1973, 1978, 1984 International Bible Society. Used by permission of Zondervan Bible Publishers.

Scripture quotations marked (RSV) are taken from the *Revised Standard Version of the Bible.* Copyright © 1946, 1952, 1971 by Division of Christian Education of the National Council of Churches in Christ in the U.S.A. Used by permission.

www.guideposts.org
1-800-431-2344
Guideposts Books & Inspirational Media Division
Developmental Editors: Cristine Bolley and Deb Strubel
Cover design by Diane Bonder
Interior design by Cindy LaBreacht
Photo by Jonelle Weaver/Photodisc Green/Getty Images
Typeset by Nancy Tardi
Printed in the United States of America

Contents

Introduction

Christmas is the most widely celebrated holiday in the world. The most popular vision of Christmas is an old-fashioned Victorian home nestled in gently falling snow, with children on toboggans or skating on a nearby lake, while a log blazes in the hearth and candles flicker all around. Ivy, holly and mistletoe are strung from every doorway. The turkey is stuffed, the stockings are hung and everyone gathers around the piano with smiles beaming on bright faces as they all sing beloved carols in harmony.

Ah . . . sounds perfect, doesn't it? Or does it? Sadly, today's Christmas sentiment goes more like this: Sleigh bells may be jingling and tree lights may be twinkling but inside my head I am screaming, "Take me away, Calgon!"

Don't despair. There is hope and some of it is right here in this book. My goal is to help you add a little peace and quiet to your holiday celebrations and make room for meaningful time with loved ones. We'll take it a step at a time, beginning with how to identify the problems that have gotten us off track. For example, if holidays seem too busy to be enjoyed, perhaps part of the problem is that you have unrealistic expectations about what events should be included. Many of us think a holiday like Christmas or Thanksgiving should bring us all closer and heal old wounds. Or we may think the holiday will be a simply marvelous time of charity and goodwill. Then we are disappointed when it falls short.

I will help you realize that this extra burden of expectation on top of our already overloaded schedules is not only stressful but can actually strain relationships as well. Have you ever argued with someone over what size tree to buy or at whose home you should celebrate? Under normal circumstances we could settle these disagreements reasonably, but because we are all suffering from frazzled nerves, small decisions become very big issues.

As we learn to have reasonable expectations, we can also concentrate on having an enjoyable holiday simply by choosing to live a stress-free moment and to break the cycle of anxiety. As we learn to focus on the good and the wonderful and adopt an attitude of gratitude, we will learn to make choices that genuinely make sense for the family and the life we have. Whether your family is a blended family, an aging family or a one-person family, you will find useful tips for creating a wonderful holiday, including new ideas for adding a little glitter to your holiday décor, easy entertaining, fun activities, better gift-giving and more—all without losing your mind or your bank account!

Be encouraged, be of good cheer, and get ready to find the real treasure of the Christmas spirit for one and all.

—*Sharon Hanby-Robie*

PART ONE

O Holy Night!

SOME PEOPLE SPELL *HOLIDAY* AS S-T-R-E-S-S, but I believe these holy days are gifts from God through which we stay connected to family and friends. After all, holidays bring people together who might otherwise drift apart completely. By taking time to evaluate what is important about these out-of-the-ordinary days, we can add purpose to these annual activities and also learn to simply enjoy this break of routine. Christmas is a time for many to celebrate the love we have for Jesus and each other. God never intended that this be a time of anxiety and overwork. Perhaps our expectations are set on the wrong ambitions. God announced peace on earth when He sent Jesus to live among us. So let's take a look at the spiritual meaning of Christmas and make plans to keep the holiday simple.

The Spiritual Meaning
of Christmas

Glory to God in the highest,

and on earth peace, good will toward men.

—LUKE 2:14 (KJV)

The story of Jesus' birth has inspired composers for more than two thousand years as they strive to recreate the song of the angels singing at the birth of the Messiah. I cannot even imagine how beautiful that sound must have been. Yet, even more beautiful is the grace-filled gift that God gave us through the birth of His Son. The *peace* on earth the angels sang of to the country shepherds is that which the Messiah gives to those on whom God bestows His grace. That peace is the true celebration of Christmas.

As Nancy Twigg says in her book, *Celebrate Simply*, "Sadly, the Good News of Christ's birth is often given only a cursory nod before moving on to what has become the *real* Christmas—receiving a windfall of presents from the jolly fellow in the red suit." Add to that the stress of overextending ourselves, our calendars and our pocketbooks, and you end up with exhaustion and chaos. As a result, most of us would simply be happy with a little bit of quiet to accompany our peace on earth.

There is hope, however, even for the weariest of Christmas spirits. Rick Warren, author of *The Purpose Driven Life*, wrote an article for *Ladies Home Journal* magazine titled, "The Purpose Driven Christmas." In it he said that there are five key purposes for Christmas: meaningful fellowship, personal growth, helpful service, joyful worship and cheerful sharing. He goes on to say that if you focus on these five purposes throughout the Christmas season, you will reduce your stress, increase your joy and experience the holiday in a far more significant way.

Jo Robinson and Jean Coppock Staeheli, authors of *Unplug the Christmas Machine*, say that we ask Christmas to do too much for us. We want it to strengthen our family bonds, give our spirits a lift, stimulate our compassion and generosity, help us get in touch with far-flung friends, confirm our deepest religious beliefs, show off our hospitality skills, establish our rank in the social order . . . the list goes on. No one celebration can do all that! They suggest a values-clarification exercise to help you decide which parts of Christmas are most worthy of your efforts. I agree with them. We can only make plans to accommodate our greatest desires when we take time to consider what is most important to us.

CHRISTMAS IS A TIME TO CELEBRATE PEOPLE WE LOVE

First we must decide with *whom* we want to have real fellowship. Worthwhile fellowship requires heart-to-heart sharing, and honest communication is necessary for family and friends to grow closer to each other. That kind of sharing cannot be orchestrated with *everyone* you know. It demands being selective with your time as well as purposefully selecting those with whom you will spend time.

When it comes to personal growth, as Rick Warren suggests, the best place to practice is within our own families. Why? Because one of the most stressful realities of holiday celebration centers around the unresolved hurts, unsettled conflicts, painful memories and uncomfortable relationships that often exist within the family. The truth is that all families are composed of imperfect people. So why on earth do we expect each other to be perfect? Rick Warren says, "We hurt one another—sometimes intentionally and sometimes not." Unless we learn to forgive, we will spend every Christmas celebrating with an underlying tension that prevents us from enjoying the gift of the season.

Christmas is a time for reconciliation. Jesus came to restore our broken relationship with God and with others. It is our job to make peace—that is the reason for the season. It is only when we have made peace with others that we can truly give thanks and celebrate in joyful worship of Jesus—the true Christmas gift—the Christ. And, as Terry Helwig wrote about for Guideposts, Jesus is the Candle of Love:

> Today is Christmas Eve. The grandfather clock in the hall dongs six times. And in the still shadows of early morning, I light the fifth candle on my Advent wreath.
>
> The fifth candle, the Christ candle, plays an important role in our church's Christmas Eve service. Late in the service, our minister takes a small, unlit candle and approaches the

altar where the Christ candle burns. Lighting his candle in its flame, he begins the passing of that flame.

I remember last year how candlelight reflected off his glasses as he carried his flame toward the two ushers waiting to pass the flame to the congregation. Rustling noises filled the pews as everyone readied their candles. My husband Jim lifted his candle toward the usher, then turned and passed his flame to our daughter Mandy, sitting beside him. Mandy tilted her candle toward me. A drop of warm wax fell on my hand as my candle burst into flame. Then I turned and edged toward the man sitting beside me. In every pew, neighbor turned to neighbor. And gradually, one by one, the entire sanctuary filled with the flickering light of two hundred tiny flames. Looking again at the Christ candle, burning serenely at the front of the church, I realized that each of us had symbolically received and passed on the love of Christ.

The powerful symbolism of that moment remains with me, even now, as I journey toward my inner Bethlehem. Staring into the flames of my Advent wreath, this Christmas Eve, I discover the sleeping candle of Christ deep within me. And as I light the Christ candle within, I know a thousand other flames can spring from it, if only I am willing to share that light.

And perhaps sharing that light is easier than I think. I remember caroling last week at the convalescent home where a frail gentleman was seated in a wheelchair in front of me. He wore a bulky gray sweater that made him look like a giraffe in elephant's clothing. His mouth gaped in a smile until a nurse unknowingly knocked off one of his navy blue slippers. She was gone before he could protest. As we sang, his black-stocking foot fished unsuccessfully on the floor for his slipper. Minutes passed. His foot kept moving. Then blushing, I stepped forward, knelt beside him and pulled the slipper onto his foot. I thought of Jesus washing the disciples' feet saying, "[I have] come not to be served but to serve" (Matthew 20:28, RSV). When I looked up, the man's grateful eyes met mine and something passed between us. I think it was the flame of the Christ candle.

It seems that the flame can be passed quite simply . . . by washing a foot or slipping on a shoe. Perhaps, as Mother Teresa said, "It is not how much we do, but how much love we put into the doing."

SIMPLICITY MADE SIMPLE

SIMPLY FORGIVE. Forgiveness is the most valuable gift we can give anyone, including ourselves. Forgiving is a lesson in growth. By forgiving we create an opportunity to grow into the kind of person God designed us to be.

Be kind. Look for opportunities to **DO SIMPLE ACTS OF KINDNESS**. The stress of the holidays leaves a lot of people operating on their last nerve. A little unexpected kindness can make a difference.

Actress Jamie Lee Curtis says, "The holidays are a time to create memories that have nothing to do with things *bought*, but only with the things taught and shared. It is in the faces and smiles and sounds of children, the weight of them against us as we cuddle up, that remind us that life is short and our time with our children is brief, that they grow up and out and away. That knowledge is what has me clinging to the holidays as **A TIME OF CONNECTION** to my family, friends and loved ones."

Worship. This is especially needed when you are feeling disconnected. Try returning to the church of your youth or attending services with friends at their church. Remember to **MAKE TIME FOR JOYFUL WORSHIP**. Caroling is a great way to spread the true spirit of Christmas to your community while experiencing a bit of it yourself at the same time.

EVALUATE WHAT IS IMPORTANT to you. Is it time to celebrate the birth of Christ? Is it time to be a peacemaker within your own family? Is it simply time to enjoy being with your immediate family? Is it time to create a beautiful and inviting home environment to share with others? Is it a time to simply exchange gifts with others? Is it a time to help those less fortunate? Or perhaps it is a time to strengthen bonds with family and friends. Or maybe it's really just time to take a break and relax. You decide!

Lord, I know that I must be at peace with others
in order to have real communion with You. Help me
to use the seasons of celebration as holy days of
reconciliation with people You have placed in my life.
May Your love always shine through mine. Amen.

Expectations

To sum up, let all be harmonious, sympathetic,
brotherly, kindhearted, and humble in spirit. . . .

—1 PETER 3:8 (NAS)

I hate fake Christmas trees, but I am seriously considering buying one anyway. I am simply tired of the annual screaming match that my hubby and I have as we attempt to position the real tree so that it stands one hundred percent straight! Part of the problem is that this is not something I can physically do myself. The other part of the problem is that it is something that my husband just doesn't have the patience for. The bigger problem is that he *insists* that we put up a tree.

Quite frankly, as much as I love the smell, look and atmosphere that a Christmas tree brings to our home, I am usually too stressed and too busy to even want to fuss with it. You see, the only part of the Christmas tree that my hubby deals with is the part we fight about—getting it into the stand. The decorating, undecorating and repacking of all the ornaments is left up to me. In addition, we spend so little time during the holidays at home that I hardly get to enjoy it at all. If I had a fake little tree that simply popped up—lights and all—it would surely take some of the stress out of this part of the holiday. But I hate fake Christmas trees. . . .

The top complaints about the holidays include the increased expectations on our time and obligations to buy gifts, go to parties and travel. This extra burden on top of our already overloaded schedules is stressful because everyone is suffering from frazzled nerves, but it also creates relationship issues (like our yearly argument over a lopsided tree). Sadly, most of us don't realize that the main problem is that our expectations for a *perfect* Christmas are simply too grand.

Neither do we realize that we have set ourselves up to be disappointed. Yes, the media and the retailers certainly play along with our silly game of unrealistic expectations, but we have choreographed our own failure since we planned the first Christmas together with our mate or our child or our grandchild. We wanted that memory to be filled with tantalizing aromas, delicious foods and beautiful decorations. And once we turned that first holiday into something unforgettable, we didn't want to disappoint our loved ones the next year. So now we continue to attempt to outdo ourselves each year. And when our sweet but now elderly parents were no longer able to contribute their part to the Christmas extravaganza, we added their list of duties to our own.

In our hearts, we are yearning for a simpler yet significant way to celebrate this special day, but we don't have any idea as to how to stop our Christmas machine. The result is as Garrison Keillor, author and public radio personality says, "The lovely thing about Christmas is that it's compulsory, like a thunderstorm, and we all go through it together."

PERFECTION ISN'T NEEDED FOR A
PERFECTLY WONDERFUL HOLIDAY

Handel H. Brown, author of *A Recipe for a Merry Christmas* and onetime pastor of the First Presbyterian Church in St. Cloud, Florida, says that "the secret of Christmas joy is love and friendliness—a love and a friendliness which are not so obvious at other times of the year." That may be true for some, but I suspect that the pressure to be loving and friendly simply adds to the stress for many people. The reality is that unless we develop realistic expectations about the holidays we will continue to be stressed and disappointed with the results.

For me, I either have to learn to be happy with a fake Christmas tree or simply accept the fact that, as long as the real tree doesn't fall down, a little leaning is just fine. The key is communicating with those you love that just as there are no perfect people, neither are there any perfect holidays—and that is perfectly okay, as Guideposts writer Elizabeth Sherrill realized.

> This is the Silent Night, the Holy Night. The night before Christmas when all through the house not a creature is stirring. When the world in solemn stillness lies to hear the angels sing.
>
> Not in our house. Here everything's astir. We have twelve overnight guests, four of them unexpected, and the phone is ringing, and the skirt I'm wearing to the midnight service has a jammed zipper and the callers at the door with gifts are the ones I forgot to get anything for. And I'm pressured and anxious and angry at myself for once again failing to hear the angelic song. O little town of Bethlehem, how still we see thee lie!

But isn't this part of the problem? That we've come to see Bethlehem this way, over the centuries: that hushed and holy manger scene painted by artists? No doubt there was a hush in heaven that night; this is what artists with their gifted vision are showing us. But in Bethlehem, I suspect it was more like pandemonium.

We have twelve extra people to house tonight; Bethlehem had additional hundreds. Could Mary and Joseph have been the only travelers lodged in that overflow space in the stable?

It's the unforeseen that upsets Christmas plans. But because of a sudden order from Rome their whole journey was unforeseen. How many painstaking preparations for the birth did Mary have to leave behind in Nazareth?

I chafe at crowded stores, but what about the press of people in those narrow streets? I've witnessed jostling, shouting market days in Israel—and those are willing crowds; two thousand years ago it would have been an angry one as well, herded together by order of a foreign dictator.

I'm distressed at what we've spent for Christmas. But I wonder—what was the price of bread in Bethlehem that night? How much did Joseph have to pay for the water Mary needed?

Silent night. Holy night. It was holy, of course, in the only place that matters—in the hearts of those who understood what was happening. But the holiness occurred in a noisy world. A tense and pressured time of history. Come, Lord Jesus, tonight, into this chaotic world of ours.

SIMPLICITY MADE SIMPLE

ADJUST YOUR PERCEPTION of perfection. Most of our ideas for the "perfect" Christmas come from what we *think* existed in holidays gone by. For example, we think that the old-fashioned Christmas is what we should be recreating. The reality is that the old-fashioned Christmas was just for children. Adults did not exchange gifts, and there wasn't the hullabaloo around making everything picture-perfect that media emulates today. In an old-fashioned Christmas, people simply enjoyed each other. The other problematic perception is the one we carry around in our heads from childhood. It's easy to remember a wonderful Christmas experience from our childhood because we didn't have to clean, shop, cook and wrap all those presents—we simply enjoyed ourselves! Recognizing that our perception might need a new pair of eyeglasses is winning half the battle to reach our goal: enjoying a simply wonderful holiday.

Sometimes we exacerbate the situation by not communicating our expectations to others. Just because we have always done something one way doesn't mean it is the only—or even the best—way to spend the holiday. **TAKE THE TIME TO TALK THINGS OVER.** Sometimes this simple act can keep everyone from being disappointed. Too often, we are afraid to talk about things because we *think* we know how people are going to react. Instead, we must give people the benefit of the doubt and explain the reasons why we want to do things differently than we have in the past. Often, when others see that we are sincere and are truly trying to make things better for everyone, they understand and support changes in tradition.

Recognize that **IT'S OKAY TO FEEL THE WAY YOU DO**. It's okay if just thinking about the holidays puts your head into a spin. Give yourself permission to feel whatever you feel—you don't have to justify emotions—they simply exist. You can, however, change your expectations, and that will often go a long way toward changing how you feel too. Don't judge yourself or compare your holiday attitude to others' feelings or actions. We are different from one another and we simply react differently to circumstances. What one person finds energizing, another can find exhausting—but even that is okay!

Don't lose your sense of humor. In times of chaos and stress, humor can be your most important resource. **LEARN TO LAUGH AT YOURSELF**—very little will ruin your day when you do.

LET GO OF PERFECTION. Only God can achieve perfection, so stop trying to compete with Him, because you won't win. It doesn't matter if there is a spot on the tablecloth—that is not what is important. The spirit of celebration and the fellowship are what matter most. My mother taught me a valuable lesson: If the house is filled with people, food and laughter, no one will notice the handprints on the wall.

Lord, You are the One Who called us to celebrate Your love. Filter my vision to see food, fun and festivities as simply a grand way to fellowship with family, regardless of how far from perfection our efforts seem. Amen.

Stress and De-stress

Look, there on the mountains, the feet of one
who brings good news, who proclaims peace! Celebrate
your festivals, O Judah, and fulfill your vows. . . .

—NAHUM 1:15 (NIV)

Nahum's proclamation of peace is complete with encouragement to celebrate our festivals. The picture that this good news creates is one of joy and complete restoration of the Lord's great plan for His people. Although this verse is not specifically about Christmas, it is a good example of how God wants us to celebrate His ordained festivals. Feasts or festivals were religious observances that conveyed *joyful* celebration—and what could be more joyous than celebrating the birth of our Lord? That is, unless we are too tired and too stressed to even smile!

Where are those "Kodak moments" that everyone talks about? Many of us hear sleigh bells jingling and see tree lights twinkling, but the shoppers are screaming and the warm greetings of the Christmas season are coming from the rising of our blood pressure! Even if we resigned ourselves to the fact that there is no such thing as a perfect holiday, it can still be stressful.

In fact, a Gallup poll of 1,001 Americans revealed that almost half of those surveyed, forty-eight percent, reported experiencing some degree of stress during the holidays, and fifty-five percent also reported losing sleep. It isn't surprising that more women than men experienced holiday-time insomnia (fifty-two percent versus thirty-eight percent respectively). In fact, women were almost twice as likely as men to report feeling "exhausted" after the holiday hustle and bustle![1]

Part of the problem is that stress has become such a part of modern life that many of us simply assume that tension and anxiety are unavoidable. Although our stress thresholds are as unique as each individual, there is a point when we do become overstressed and exceed our coping capabilities. The sheer number of demands made on us during the holiday season is more than most of us can handle without feeling overwhelmed. As our stress response is engaged over and over again with no time for rest, our warm feelings of goodwill toward man quickly turn to competition over the last parking space in the lot!

STRESS IS SELF-CREATED

What most of us don't realize is that we are the source of our own stress. We have the ability to control stress simply by the choices we make. Yes, stress is an option that we choose in processing these unpleasant events. For example, how you choose to react is up to you when stuck in line behind someone who can't find her checkbook and also needs to have each gift packaged separately while going through the receipt to verify that she received all the applicable discounts. You can either blame the person in front of you for the stress you feel and make matters worse, *or* you can remind yourself that you are choosing to live a stress-free moment and break the cycle of anxiety by taking a deep breath and pushing the negative attitude and thoughts from your mind.

Instead, choose to concentrate on how enjoyable the holiday is going to be with your family and be grateful that you are not as problematic or compulsive as the one standing in line in front of you. Adopting an attitude of gratitude will make it impossible to be stressed as Pam Kidd, writer for Guideposts, has found:

> On this fourth Sunday of Advent, the house is decorated, the presents wrapped. As my son Brock says, "It's time to kick back and enjoy Christmas."
>
> But earlier today, instead of "kicking back," I willingly entered the mayhem of commercial Christmas. After church, I went to the most hectic of all holiday places, the mall. Everywhere there were lights and glitter, elves and big, colored balls. The music was loud. At Santa's village, kids stood in a long line. An older lady looked at me and smiled. A young mother laughed as a saleslady scooped up her child and set her right in the middle of a teddy bear display. Several people gathered around, delighted with this sight. They exchanged pleasantries as I went on.
>
> "May I help you?" a young man asked when I reached a department store. I explained my need for a tie, and the clerk made suggestions until one was chosen. "Have a great

Christmas!" he said. Later, in the gift-wrap line, the spirit was the same. Smiles, and laughter, and "Happy holidays!"

Every year, I purposely save a bit of my shopping until right before Christmas because I love the rush, the feel, the way people who usually don't even look to the right or to the left look straight at me and smile. The spirit of Christmas shows us what our world would look like if we followed Jesus' lead every day to love, love, love.

So before this Christmas passes, go to the mall or to some gathering place. Take a bag of smiles and give them to everyone you meet. The spirit of Christmas is waiting for you.

SIMPLICITY MADE SIMPLE

GET ENOUGH SLEEP. A. Christopher Hammon, director of the Center for Sleep and Stress on the Web says, "This [sleep] is one of the most overlooked secrets for coping with stress. Getting the sleep we need plays a key role in the amount of stress we can handle through the day before becoming overstressed. It is during sleep that our brain sorts through information taken in through the day, and works toward resolving emotional issues that have come up."[2] Experts have also discovered that getting as little as an hour less sleep than we need affects how we function in the course of a day, creating situations that contribute significantly to our stress. Plan to eat moderately; especially avoid overeating at night. Make time for exercise. Most people tend to reduce or even stop their workout regimens during the holidays despite the fact that we know that exercise is one of the best available stress reducers and sleep enhancers.

GET ORGANIZED. Do as much as you can as early as you can. Start by identifying the things you *want* to do and the things you *need* to do. Then prioritize the list. Once organized, you can manage and budget your time to accommodate what really matters.

Make a stress list. Hammon found such a list to be helpful. By identifying specific stressors that are unique to each of us, such as certain people, events or situations, we can intentionally **AVOID KNOWN STRESS INDUCERS**. Awareness reduces the power that situations hold over us. Rather than simply responding with stress, we can prepare ourselves to avoid an automatic response. The more we understand our reactions to the people and situations that cause us stress the more creative and productive our reactions become.

Accept the reality that **YOU CANNOT CONTROL OR CHANGE PEOPLE**. Dr. Morton C. Orman, who specializes in teaching people how to eliminate stress, says, "When people don't behave as we want during the holidays, we often set out to change or control their behavior. When we fail to accomplish this goal, we end up feeling angry and frustrated. Thus, it's not just the behavior of others that drives us crazy during the holidays, but rather that people fail to think, feel, or behave exactly as we want."[3] The answer to this problem is simply *not* to try to control other people! If Aunt Edna always gets drunk and makes a fool of herself—there is nothing you can do except change your attitude. Consider it your gift to her.

TALK TO YOUR FAMILY. You may find that the truth of the matter is that the big extravaganza you are planning really doesn't matter as much as you think it does to the people who love you. Or you may learn that something that is effortless on your part is what your family is hoping to experience during the holiday. Rather than letting the external events spoil your mood, take a break and enjoy the season with your family a little more. Give yourself permission to simply relax rather than taking on the responsibility of making every moment better for everybody else.

Lord, I choose to enjoy the rush of wanting to do
as much as possible for others, but I promise
to lay aside anxiety over what is left undone in order
to truly rest in the joy of Your love. Amen.

Traditions

And the Lord spake unto Moses and Aaron in the land

of Egypt, saying, This month shall be unto you the

beginning of months: it shall be the first month

of the year to you. Speak ye unto all the congregation

of Israel, saying, In the tenth day of this month they

shall take to them every man a lamb, according to the

house of their fathers, a lamb for an house.

—EXODUS 12:1–3 (KJV)

P assover was a holiday designed by God Himself to celebrate Israel's deliverance from Egypt and to remind the people of what God had done for them. Today, holidays act as annual reminders of what God has done for us. The traditions surrounding our holidays give families a sense of belonging and tie us together.

Tevya, the father from the musical *Fiddler on the Roof*, also believed that traditions helped families stay connected as he sang about the importance of them

---

in his life—and so too should we believe and use traditions to help us stay connected. Developing family traditions to highlight the religious significance of certain holidays serves as a reminder to our elders and a learning experience for the younger ones. But there is more.

Barbara H. Fiese published an article that summarized fifty years of research at Syracuse University regarding family rituals and traditions. They found that the symbolic nature of family rituals provided a sense of belonging and personal identity—aspects, they say, that are important for our health and well-being as individuals. "Rituals (traditions) involve symbolic communication and convey 'this is who we are' as a group. There is an effective commitment that leaves the individual feeling that the activity has a felt rightness that provides a sense of belonging. Furthermore, there is often an emotional residue where once the act is completed, the individual may replay it in memory to recapture some of the affective experience. Rituals and traditions also provide continuity in meaning across generations with the anticipation for repeat performance and an investment that 'this is how our family will continue to be.' When rituals are disrupted, there is a threat to group cohesion."[4]

TRADITIONS GIVE US STABILITY

Without a doubt, family traditions are very important in providing the sense of togetherness we all yearn for, especially during the holiday season. In addition, traditions strengthen family relationships and provide emotional stability while maintaining family contact. Traditions also are a wonderful opportunity for creating memorable moments. Even teens agree.

When teenagers were asked their opinions about traditions, there was a strong positive attitude toward maintaining family traditions. Teen Aaron Cobb wrote about his opinion for *About.com*, saying, "These traditions have added continuity to my life—connecting the person who I have become throughout the years with the Aaron of yesteryear. They have added consistency to my life—drawing me back to the truly important aspects of life every year—without fail. They have added coherence to my life—giving me vision for the future and the life that is in store."[5]

Another teen writes, "When I was a kid, on Christmas morning, we would all line up on the stairs and go down together. When I returned one year after I had been an adult for a long time, my three siblings and I still insisted on 'calling' our place on the stairs and giggled like little kids. We felt silly, but it was the right thing for us to do."[6]

As important as traditions are, they don't have to be complicated. Carole Carroll, an associate professor of sociology at Middle Tennessee State University, says that "research regarding the social benefits of traditions show it doesn't seem to matter what the tradition is, only that it is practiced." Senior psychologist Tyler Henson says, "We always have a massive pot of mashed potatoes and we usually sit around and sing for a couple of hours."[7]

But even the most cherished traditions can sometimes, due to circumstances or limitations of time, lose their shine and get a little lackluster. When they do, don't be afraid to give them some sprucing up. Although change is hard, it can be good, as Guideposts writer Marilyn Moore found out:

> I was feeling blue about how Christmas had changed. Mother was in a nursing home in Wisconsin, my children were grown and living away from home, I was alone in Connecticut. There

would be no stockings hung, no oranges in the toes—a tradition in our family from my mother's childhood on a farm. On Christmas Eve there, neighboring farm families would gather at the old Zion Church. After carols, recitations and Bible readings, one of the farmers, dressed as Santa Claus, would give each child a gift—an orange. Before the age of air transport and refrigeration fresh oranges were a delicacy, especially at Christmastime, when their golden glow must have seemed like a light of hope to those Welsh immigrants struggling through a hard Wisconsin winter.

After mother married my father, she continued the custom and my sisters, brother and I always found oranges in the toes of our Christmas stockings. Somehow Mother kept alive the Christmas wonder of her childhood. Later, I would put oranges in my own children's stocking. But now, what would happen to the tradition?

Then when I received the crate of oranges my friend had sent from Florida I got the new idea . . .

For three days and nights I worked on the oranges, slicing them and boiling them with sugar. I sterilized glasses and the steam filled the house and billowed out into the cold winter air. Finally, there lined up on the windowsill, were gleaming glasses filled with marmalade. New gifts and a new tradition! Here was one for Mother . . . there's some for the neighbors . . . these will be for the children . . . oh, merry, merry, Christmas!

If you're feeling blue about some changes this Christmas, maybe you need to find something new to hold your wonder. You've heard the saying: turn lemons into lemonade. *Or, oranges into marmalade!*

Isn't *new* life what the Christmas message is all about?

SIMPLICITY MADE SIMPLE

Slow the Christmas blur by **TAKING TIME FOR TRADITIONS**. If your holiday seasons feel like you are running on "fast-forward," create a new tradition to slow them down. It is only when you punctuate what is important that others will take notice the way they should. Consider establishing a special nightly devotion just for the Christmas season.

LEARN TO COMPROMISE during transition times. Whether you are a newlywed, divorced or have just moved into your first apartment, this is a time your traditions may need a little tweaking. For newlyweds: the number one rule is, don't fight about how to celebrate. A fight is not how you want to remember your first Christmas together. Instead, consider mixing a little of his tradition along with yours. Just because your family has *always* done it a certain way doesn't necessarily mean it's the only way. In fact, when circumstances change, you have the opportunity to keep some of the old traditions and make new ones.

KEEP CHILDREN INVOLVED. It is especially helpful to have a "tradition" that is timed to happen after all the gifts have been opened. Children need some way to occupy that time. One family started a ritual of decorating a tree for wild birds. They placed the tree outdoors close to a window so all the children could watch, and the birds enjoyed their special treat. They used unsalted peanuts in shells, strung with heavy-duty thread, apple pieces, beef suet, peanut butter dipped bread crumbs, rice cakes and popcorn. When I was young, my family tradition called upon all the children up to age sixteen to create a skit or play. Immediately following dinner, we went to the basement and prepared for our show. It was a very big deal to all of us children— we felt so important and excited that the adults would be giving us their full attention for the performance.

Focus on the spiritual. **MAKE SURE TO INCLUDE SPIRITUAL TRADITIONS** that will bring your family closer to God. Some of the simplest acts include praying together, attending services together, and reading sacred writings or Bible stories together.

EVALUATE YOUR OLD TRADITIONS. To make sure your traditions are still working for your family, it's a good idea to occasionally identify and decide whether or not what you are doing continues to be significant to those involved. I recently asked my goddaughter about holiday traditions and their importance to her. She said, sadly, that at this point in her life, none of the old traditions are working for her because her parents are now divorced. If she could have her "dream tradition," it would be her entire family together for the Christmas celebration. Since she recently moved into her own apartment, this would be a very good year to help her establish a new and meaningful tradition of her own.

Dream a little. Most of us spend too much time trying to make Christmas resemble something from the idealized past. Perhaps it is time to **INITIATE A NEW WAY TO CELEBRATE**. One family, at Grandma's suggestion, chose to rent a beach house together. Instead of slaving in the kitchen while bored teenagers complained and husbands watched football, she and her whole family had a great time at the beach! Jo Robinson and Jean Coppock Staeheli, authors of *Unplug the Christmas Machine*, suggest that simplifying the celebration does not have to take away any of its value. In fact, they believe that by creating a new vision for holiday celebrations, you help to remove the burden while providing an opportunity for real joy. "Taking the time to create the fantasy is one of the most important steps you can take. Your fantasies can give you a new enthusiasm for Christmas and the sense of direction you need to start building a better celebration."

Father, You are wise to ask us to pause and celebrate the birth of Jesus. Our traditions will be examined by generations to come. Help me to establish holiday rituals that will always point to our love for You. Amen.

PART TWO

'Tis the Season to Be Jolly

HOLIDAYS ARE ABOUT PEOPLE—and often people who we haven't seen the entire year will invite us to participate in their celebrations. But it is right to put your immediate family first. In this section, we will look at the value of holding a family meeting and letting everyone contribute ideas to how the holidays should be enjoyed. This is especially important to newly blended families, or individuals who face their first holiday without their spouse or loved one celebrating with them. God has a plan to make all things new, even the old traditions that cannot be celebrated exactly as they were in years gone by. It can even be tempting to pull away and avoid conflicting traditions of other family members and friends, but God's goal for us is peace and harmony with others. It's simple: Always put people first and you will please the heart of God as you celebrate the holidays.

Holiday Family Stress

The Lord then said to Noah, "Go into the ark,

you and your whole family. . . ."

—GENESIS 7:1 (NIV)

When it comes to spending time with our families during the holidays, it can sometimes feel like we are expected to set off together on the ark. How would you and your family fare if God commanded you to confine yourselves to a boat for a few months? And don't forget all the animals that were also on this little cruise. The noise, the smell, the chaos—all adding to the family festival of stress! That's how it is for some families. Instead of enjoying one another, they have more disagreements and feel overwhelmed. Perhaps it is because there are so many decisions to make and extra activities to schedule. Add to that the worries of finances, and holidays can bring out the worst in even the best families.

Just because we love each other doesn't mean that spending Christmas together is the best thing to do. There is no commandment that says you must spend your holiday by ducking potshots from your Uncle George about the way you dress or how you spend your money. It makes far more sense to consider family problems when planning gatherings.

For example, if you know that certain family members do not get along well, take the time to resolve the situation before you get together. Christmas dinner is *not* the time to make up. And leaving things to chance often causes more problems and makes things worse. The mere fact that you are already dreading the family holiday together is a telltale sign things are not going to go well. Stop and think about it: the key thing to keep in mind is that a lot of the stress surrounding the holidays is preventable.

PREPARE FOR THE BEST EXPERIENCE

Relationship expert Keith Varnum says that there are simple strategies that will not only help you survive the traditional family holiday visit but also enable you to actually enjoy it! He says, "The Boy Scouts motto, 'Be Prepared!' has never been more helpful than when going to visit the family at the holidays." He encourages forming alliances with brothers and sisters and other relatives who are sympathetic to your plight. It can be as simple as agreeing to run interference for each other. Varnum even suggests that you "hold mock question and answer sessions with your allies to practice gracefully fending off the slings and arrows. Prepare for cross-examination." That way you will have your answers ready for the questions you know you are sensitive or touchy about.[8]

The best defense is always a good offense. Prepare a list of questions to be used as responses to throw Uncle George off the subject. If you and your younger sister are still fighting over childhood rivalries, adopt a bit of humor and dance around the old land mine instead of walking into it. It's also a good idea to have an exit strategy ready just in case conversations get too heated.

Warn your family in advance that you might have to cut your visit short. It is far better to be honest about how much time you can actually spend with your family and still enjoy them than it is to end up bored and bothered, or filled with resentful feelings.

Set a realistic expectation. Sometimes the reality is that the best we can hope for is "surviving" the holiday rather than getting everyone to be happy about it. Keith Varnum recommends that we "be of good cheer, the end is near! You only have to dodge the bullets of family expectations once a year—and you don't have to stay any longer than you can keep on top of the ruckus. Be lighthearted, playful and flexible—and enjoy the family circus as much as you can!"

Watch for danger signs, especially between you and your immediate family. If you and your spouse find that you are retreating from each other or are being irritable about everything, schedule some quiet time together to talk about it. Even fifteen minutes can make a difference. Other danger signs include a defensive attitude, being overtired, sleeping too much, forgetfulness, not eating well or feeling sad or depressed. We all need to know our limits and do only what we can. It's okay to say *no*. It's also a good idea to realize that this is simply one "season." It is not going to last a lifetime—although the memories may. Instead of looking at all that is wrong, look at all you have accomplished and how well things are going. That's what Guideposts writer Carol Kuykendall did.

During the first week of December, I usually start feeling fatigued by all my Christmas preparations and obligations. Last year, however, a talk I heard at church gave me a new burst of energy.

"Every year we vow things will be different," the speaker said, "and every year we find ourselves facing the same responsibilities. The truth is we can't change many of our Christmas obligations, but we can change our attitudes by remembering *why* we're doing all these things. Christmas gives us opportunities to show our love."

Just before she sat down the speaker quoted a line from Victor Hugo's *Les Misérables* that became the theme of my Christmas preparation: "To love another is to see the face of God."

A few days later, when my sister called unexpectedly from California to say she and her family could join us over Christmas, I didn't think about the extra obligations that lay ahead. I thought about the great *opportunity* for a four-day family reunion: the *opportunity* to come up with unique gift ideas, which led to the *opportunity* to sort through a huge box of old photos and make an album for each family, telling the chronological story of our childhood Christmases.

From that point forward, while my days were full, they were not draining. And as these acts of love became *opportunities*, I felt energized. When finally we all were gathered together on Christmas Day, eating and exchanging gifts, I looked at the radiant faces around the room and realized that bringing happiness to someone else is like gazing into the eyes of Jesus . . . and seeing the face of God.

SIMPLICITY MADE SIMPLE

Put your immediate family first. It is more important to meet the needs of your spouse and children than to make sure that grouchy old uncle is happy. Be flexible with your spouse. Some traditions are definitely worth fighting for—but you may be able to let others go. **HAVE A FAMILY MEETING** and let everyone participate in choosing how you will celebrate the holidays. Talk openly with one another about your expectations, hopes and fears.

DON'T TRAVEL OUT OF GUILT. Travel today is simply not fun. Expecting children and even the elderly to fare well through the stress of security screening, packed airplanes or busy holiday traffic is unrealistic. Don't be afraid to have an honest talk with family far away about how difficult it is for you to make a trip during the holidays. Suggest visiting at a more convenient time.

Keep kids occupied. Whether you are traveling or simply spending the afternoon with nearby family, be sure to **GIVE THE CHILDREN PLENTY TO DO**. Cindy Turner of Chino Hills, California, suggests giving each child a roll of quarters. If there is any fighting or complaining, after one warning the offender(s) must deposit a quarter into the piggy bank. When they reach their destination, the kids get to keep the quarters they have left for spending money.[9]

TAKE MENTAL HEALTH BREAKS. Keith Varnum says to take strategic time-outs. For example, when you feel you are reaching your limit of being able to cope with family judgment and scrutiny, that is the perfect time for a break. He suggests going to the bathroom and splashing your face with water. Or going outside and getting a breath of fresh air. Take a short walk and let nature revive you. Or, better yet, make yourself look like a real good guy by volunteering to run errands, wash dishes or even empty the trash.

Father, sometimes loving others seems impossible.
Yet, in Your wisdom, You ask us to love others
as we do You. Help me to see Your eyes
in theirs, and be Your face to them. Amen.

Blended Families

"Your people will be my people and your God my God."

—RUTH 1:16 (NIV)

R uth's promise to her mother-in-law Naomi is important in many ways, but it is most relevant for those who find themselves in a blended family. Ruth is not only a widow, but she is also a Moabite, a different tribe than Naomi's, and Ruth was raised with a different belief system too. But she chose to identify with her mother-in-law, and by doing so she also identified herself with God's covenanted people. Through alliance with His people, Ruth established her claim to a relationship with God.

Eventually, Ruth is blessed for her loyalty to her new family with marriage to Boaz. Ruth asks Boaz to cover her with his cloak—symbolizing the protection of marriage. Ruth's faith in the Lord made it possible for her to be an ancestor of David and, eventually, the Messiah. When God chose to work through a Moabitess (Ruth), He showed that the new covenant would be for *all* people who believed, not just for the Hebrew people.

This is significant because it is a wonderful example of how blended families should work. Combining families necessitates combining lifestyles. For children and adults, this creates all kinds of personal losses, especially in the area of sacred traditions. Just as Ruth had to let go of her past traditions in order to become part of Naomi's family, blended families need to let go of some past traditions in order to create cohesiveness within the new family unit.

This process of creating new customs is difficult for many children who have already relinquished their original idea of family tradition when their parents divorced. After they reestablished themselves with one parent, a new set of attitudes and beliefs was adopted. If a new marriage happens, changing those ideas to create *yet another* set of family traditions can bring about deep mourning among all members of a newly combined family. Despite the happiness of new relationships, a former way of life is lost along with the comfort of all that was familiar.

Parents cannot expect their children to simply be grateful for a new two-parent family. Taube S. Kaufman, author of *The Combined Family* and a licensed clinical social worker, says, "Children who have experienced the end of one family are often reluctant to settle into a new family living situation. If children have experienced the death of a parent, they know that nothing lasts forever, and if they have lived through divorce, they know that if one marriage can end, so can another. And, if they trust, and are disappointed again, could they bear the pain?"

Nearly everyone knows a blended family who is trying to reform their family unit. The first few holiday seasons for stepfamilies will be the most difficult simply because, in the beginning, all combined families do not look or feel like a "real" family. And that is okay—because the truth is that new family members do not share a common history or a mutual definition of how families interact. In fact, the first few holidays may even be a disaster as tempers flare and tensions grow, and most of the family will simply be relieved when the entire event is over! Some families will try to be so inclusive that the children end up with three turkeys to eat at Thanksgiving, and six different homes to visit over Christmas. It's exhausting!

MAKE ROOM IN YOUR HEART FOR CHANGE

Despite our best efforts, this time of expectation for family togetherness cannot be met by the new configuration of stepfamilies. Many children, during the holiday season, will be reminded of the loss they experienced when their biological family separated. They may also have conflicting feelings about the creation of this new family. Even the parents will face the loss of the biological family unit when they have to "share" their children during the holiday season. As a result, the holidays may produce more melancholy and less cheer than any other season. Acknowledging this reality is important for keeping expectations real.

Taube Kaufman says, "Because some members of newly formed combined families retain complex ties to previous marriages, any or all of these members may find themselves in a situation in which many new people have been added to their lives. These newcomers, however, do not necessarily fit into any societally recognized pattern. Remarried parents, their former spouses and new spouses, the parents and relatives of these people, and even the offspring of outside parents and their new spouses—all of these people can intrude on combined family life."

It's easy to see how disagreements can arise as family celebrations bring ex-family members face-to-face with their worst fears. Finding a balance within the new family is critical not only for holiday seasons, but also for the future well-being of the new family.

Accepting the fact that most blended families can take seven to eight years to really blend is difficult, but it's true. That's why it is important to negotiate new family traditions despite the fact that they will require a tremendous amount of give and take. Everyone should anticipate feeling a sense of loss as new ways of celebrating holidays and other important events are established. But it will be worth it because the new set of values and traditions is what will define who you are and what you mean to each other as a new family. By borrowing from the old family patterns and creating new ones, you will build a new alliance—just as Ruth and Naomi did. And it is this new commonality of experience that will allow each member of the family to feel included, to know what to expect from others and to have a sense of history that all can share. Psychologist Patricia Papernow calls this "strengthening of middle ground." I like that expression because it removes the competition between whom and what is most important. The strengthening of middle ground will grow over time—and the sense of family will increase.

S I M P L I C I T Y   M A D E   S I M P L E

DEVELOP A SOLID COUPLE BOND. This is one of the most critical areas for the new family. If you are part of a blended family, you will feel the strain of being pulled between your own children and the new ones. It will be hard to remain steadfast and loyal to the needs of children who have already endured such loss and change without compromising your new relationship.

Offer your children constant reassurance that they are loved and valued. But also recognize that it is by the strength of your new relationship as a couple that your family stands or falls. Your whole family is depending on this relationship making it.

CREATE A PARENTING COALITION if at all possible. Remarried parents must establish a working relationship with the outside parent to resolve issues and plan holidays. Avoid power struggles to ensure open lines of communication between households, and resist the temptation to recruit children in such a struggle. The survival of the combined family also depends on the ability of "ex" family members to resolve conflicts and the willingness of its members to work together without getting hurt. In other words, it will be difficult for your new spouse to stay out of the "emotional conflict" simply because he cares for you. If you and your ex cannot resolve conflicts, you may find yourself turning to your new spouse for support. That can lead to additional problems and conflicts, which will only compound the challenges of the holiday celebration.

Be sensitive to your children's needs to be with both of their biological parents. My friend Jan found that the simplest way to solve this dilemma was to invite her ex and his girlfriend to join in their family celebration dinner. She also invited her husband's parents, making it a very large celebration. But by including everyone, it made the holiday less stressful and met most expectations. **ENCOURAGE EXPRESSION OF FEELINGS.** Let the children, grandparents and others share their feelings. Listen sensitively and avoid trying to "fix" emotions.

GIVE YOURSELF TIME to become a family. Simply getting married does not make two families become one. Acknowledge the holiday confusion and conflicts. Talk about each other's uncertainties without guilt. Keep your sense of humor and laugh about these situations if you can. When compromises aren't forthcoming, put your marriage first. Accept that finding what works for you and your family takes time and experience. Keeping a focus on the joy of your new marriage enhances your ability to cope. Practice what works, and change what does not.

PLAN AHEAD. You can't avoid the inevitable—so face the fact that the first few years of holiday seasons may be difficult. Discuss options and plan in advance by encouraging family members to share their ideas for celebrating. Avoid overcommitment and rise above animosity. Remain calm and level-headed even if challenged! And, most importantly, enjoy your family's uniqueness. Remember, this is the perfect opportunity to practice love.

> Lord, I am thankful that You adopted me into Your family, and taught me new ways of living, loving and relating to others. Help us continue to expand our family relationships to reflect the unity that You want us to have. Amen.

Interfaith Celebrations

C hrist's ethic of love does not abandon the rules, but shifts the focus of attention from one's actions to the intentions of the heart. With His sin-free life
and sacrificial death, Jesus kept perfectly both the letter *and* the spirit of the law.
Although it is impossible for us to absolutely follow the letter of the law, we can
attempt to follow Christ's lead in adhering to the "spirit" of the law in our holiday celebrations—especially for interfaith marriages. Shifting our focus to the
good intentions behind the acts of others could be a very fine idea for everyone,
especially families with two faiths.

"Holidays are one of the most stressful times for interfaith families. Along
with events such as weddings, baby namings and coming-of-age ceremonies, the
holidays are the most emotional and tradition-laden times to be navigated," says

Joan C. Hawxhurst, editor of *Dovetail*, the national periodical for Jewish/ Christian families, and the author of *The Interfaith Family Guidebook*.[10] The reason is that both partners have very specific and often deeply held ideas about how each holiday should be celebrated.

My first husband, to whom I was married for twenty years, was an agnostic. Holidays were difficult for us because they were simply a secular celebration for him. His family used this time as an opportunity for vacationing. As a Christian, Christmas and Easter were especially important religious holidays for me that involved very specific family traditions. We never had children, so I can only imagine how much more complicated things would have been if we did.

As adults, we could learn to respect each other's differences without it becoming a threat to my faith. But when interfaith marriages reach the child-bearing years, life gets more difficult. Children ask questions—a lot of questions. In fact, it is their best and favorite activity. If you have not thoroughly thought through what is most important about each of your beliefs and your traditions, you can find yourself blindsided by your children's inquiring minds. For children, the various ways their friends celebrate holidays can be confusing, and when their parents disagree on certain rituals, they are left bewildered.

Some people believe that children of interfaith families are more blessed to have the better of two faiths. Yet, others believe that it can bring about a dilution of both faiths, leaving a child with nothing of substance. I will not pretend to know who is right, but I hope to offer some insight into *celebrating* the holidays in an interfaith family.

Mary Helene Rosenbaum, award-winning coauthor of *Celebrating Our Differences: Living Two Faiths in One Marriage*, suggests that the difficulty interfaith couples have with the winter holidays often "really has to do with defining what parts of the celebrations are actually religious and which are cultural and nostalgic." We can waste a lot of time and effort arguing over insignificant symbols or traditions that do not have a foundation in or any influence over our sacred beliefs. By taking the time to identify how we see each of these traditions and symbols, we can focus on what is most essential. When making choices, it is important that each of you feels that your favorite holidays have been celebrated properly. You should also be sure that the celebration is something that both you and your partner participate in. By discovering aspects of the holidays that you both enjoy, the entire family can celebrate together. This creates a strong sense of unity rather than division.

WEAVE A FAMILY TAPESTRY OF FAITH

It is also important to keep the celebration within a comfort level that is compatible with the other's religion. For example, if your husband is Jewish, he may feel that having a Christmas tree or manger in his home is a betrayal of his own religion. One woman found a solution to this dilemma that evolved over fifteen years. She sees three threads that weave together to form what she feels is a beautiful, comforting and inspirational blanket that wraps together and warms her whole family during the winter holidays.

One thread is Hanukkah with its inspiring themes of freedom, miracles and faithfulness to one's values in the face of opposition. The second thread is Christmas, which leads to thoughts of how Christ is present in the world today, what it means to be human, and how we can work for peace and goodwill toward all. The third and final thread of this family "blanket" is all the secular influences of the season, which creates fond childhood memories for her children. But she is clear not to confuse the secular with the religious. She doesn't want her children's religious beliefs reduced to or mistaken for the secular symbols.

Hawxhurst says parents in interfaith families should prepare for the winter holidays by explaining to the children how a family's actions and observations of Christmas and Hanukkah complement each other. David Heller, author of *Talking to Your Child About God: A Book for Families of All Faiths*, offers what he holds to be the most crucial element in interfaith parenting: "You and your spouse must believe in your compatibility and in your harmony with God. And you should convey these ideas to your child. There is nothing more reassuring for an interfaith child than a solid and meaningful parental relationship."[11]

In other words, you must know what you believe in and follow through on it in what you do. Interfaith couples must do some serious thinking and negotiating to create a family plan for holiday celebrations that meets the needs of both parents and, more importantly, provides for the emotional and spiritual well-being of their children. This can be a lifelong process. But so is the walk to maturity. We don't know what kind of bumps in the road we will encounter until we get there. In the meantime, we must agree that to love one another we must be willing to respect each other's spiritual beliefs.

SIMPLICITY MADE SIMPLE

MAKE A DECISION about your religious identity. Most experts agree that the simplest situation *for children* is for the parents to agree to raise the children in one faith and one set of traditions. That can be easier said than done.

What will you do if you later find that you can't live with that decision? Are you willing to renegotiate? Knowing in advance how important this is to you is critical to maintaining your original position.

TRY SOMETHING FROM BOTH HOLIDAYS. There is no one single way to celebrate. Every family has its own way of celebrating even if they have only one set of religious beliefs. Try buying a Christmas tree *and* lighting a menorah. Consider trying different approaches until you find a way that simply makes sense for you and your family. Then make it *your* tradition!

TALK ABOUT YOUR DIFFERENCES *before* you have children. It's tough enough just making it work between two parents. Couples who have talked about their religious differences and how to resolve them are better able to handle the demands of the holiday season than those who put it off. The longer you wait, the harder it will be.

USE THE BIRTHDAY PARTY ANALOGY. Just as we celebrate a family member's birthday because it is his or her day, we can celebrate holidays that one family member feels strongly about even if the others do not feel so attached. Several experts say that the best way to explain the different holidays and celebrations to children is to use this approach: Explain that you are going to help Daddy celebrate *his* holiday with a Christmas tree—you can have presents, sing carols and decorate the tree—the goal simply being to help Daddy enjoy the day. Then you will do the same for Mommy when it's her holiday. June Horowitz, an associate professor in the psychiatric/mental health department at Boston College's School of Nursing, leads counseling groups and worship for interfaith families. She says she encourages families to participate in family traditions. "A Jewish child learning about Christmas is not going to change his identity."

Focus on common themes. Celebrate similarities rather than focusing on what makes the holiday preferences different. For example, all religious and cultural holidays have some element of peace, harmony and reconciliation. You can also **HONOR THE DIFFERENCES BY EMBRACING THE COMMON *VALUES*** and how they relate to your family.

AVOID BEING COMPETITIVE. This is so important. Honor your commitment to coordinate and respect the common wishes of both parents—even after their death.

PUT YOUR FAMILY AND YOUR CHILDREN FIRST when it comes to extended family. You can't blame grandparents for wanting to share *their* holidays with the grandchildren. However, you must set boundaries and be firm about them. Whatever you and your spouse agree to in terms of holiday celebrations must be respected by your extended family. Be prepared to abandon some traditions in order to accomplish this. Inform your families early on as to the things that you will participate in and those that you will not. Don't give in under pressure. This is *your* family and *your* decision. Simply remind your family members that the holidays are a time of peace and harmony and that your goal is to create a positive experience. The best technique for avoiding explosive differences is a lot of communication with a good helping of humor!

> Lord, help me to balance respect for others with my deep sense of faith in You. Help me to demonstrate through the holidays the reality of what I believe in a way that draws others to want to know You more. Amen.

Celebrating the Holidays Alone

He seldom reflects on the days of his life, because God
keeps him occupied with gladness of heart.

—ECCLESIASTES 5:20 (NIV)

Many people find themselves alone for the holidays. Statistics indicate that over twenty-five million people in the United States live alone. We can be surrounded by people and still feel alone. However, just because we are sometimes alone doesn't mean we have to be lonely or sad. Indeed, it is quite possible to be alone and not be lonely or sad. For those of us devoted to God, we need not brood over the past or worry about the future. This should be especially comforting for those finding themselves alone for the first time during the holidays, whether due to divorce, death or distance. God truly wants to fill our hearts with joy even during the holidays spent apart from loved ones.

The holidays can seem bleak when the sights, sounds and aromas begin to remind you of past celebrations with family and friends. You may be tempted to simply not participate and let the holidays pass you by. Or you may decide to change your holiday traditions or decline invitations, thinking it will help you avoid painful memories. That strategy may leave you feeling worse, not better. Making the most of the holidays is a matter of attitude. If you choose to stay home and not find ways to mark the season, you will very likely find yourself feeling sadder and lonelier than ever.

Continuing traditions and celebrations can help you cope with stress and unpleasant feelings. In fact, traditions provide comfort and stability in times of loss and chaos. The holiday season can generate fond memories if you let it. But if you have suffered the loss of someone since the last time you celebrated a holiday, realize ahead of time that the season will now be different. Acknowledging your loss is important. Some holidays are for celebrating while some are also set aside for remembering, and that includes grieving. It's not only okay to grieve—it's important to grieve. Ignoring your grief will not make it disappear.

Give yourself the freedom to feel rather than block difficult emotions. But remember you are in charge—not your emotions. Learn from your feelings, but don't let negative emotions dominate you. As time passes, your pain will soften. Eventually, fond memories will comfort and lift you. You must let the Holy Spirit help you take the best of the past into a new future.

NURTURE YOURSELF

Your energy level will be different if the holiday is filled with memories that make you sad. For most of us, grief lowers our energy level. Therefore, it is important to avoid being overly busy, and be sure to make opportunities for getting some extra rest. Practice self-care to enhance your healing process. That means eating healthy foods, getting exercise, resting and talking to someone you trust about your feelings.

By taking care of yourself physically, emotionally and spiritually, you will make your holidays more enjoyable and relaxed. Letting friends and family know how you feel and how you are planning to celebrate (or not celebrate) is critical to letting them help you through the season. It also takes the pressure off them. It's hard for family and friends to know just what to do when someone they love is going through the loss of someone who was close to them. By taking the direct approach of communicating with them, you make it easier for yourself and everyone else too.

Give yourself a break and use this time for reflection. While seemingly everyone is racing around the shopping mall and stressing about spending too much money and not having enough time, you can create a golden opportunity to simply unwind, reflect and let the Lord comfort you.

Allow yourself to respond to your own impulses without forcing yourself to do or act in a specific way. In time, you will be able to embrace your new life. John 16:22 (NIV) says, "Now is your time of grief, but I will see you again and you will rejoice, and no one will take away your joy." Patricia Lorenz discovered this truth herself:

> That year Christmas looked bleak. I had just become a newly single parent and was facing life alone. For the first time ever, one of my children wouldn't be with me on Christmas: Jeanne, my oldest, was a foreign-exchange student in Yugoslavia. Then the annual New Year's Eve get-together in Illinois with my relatives, to which I had been looking forward, had been canceled. And it was my turn to host the huge neighborhood Christmas party.
>
> But here's what happened that week: On Christmas Eve, my other three children all wanted to attend the traditional

family service at our church. Later, they insisted upon another family tradition: reading the Christmas story from the Bible before we opened presents. At midnight, my friends Bob and Betsy whisked me off to the candlelight service at their church. Two days later, they offered to co-host the neighborhood party, and all the neighbors pitched in to help with the refreshments. Then on New Year's weekend, my out-of-town family came to my home, ending the holiday week with loads of laughter and love.

Because I gave in to the gentle nudgings and invitations of friends and family, that Christmas week became a memory I treasure. Sometimes it's hard to get through the Christmas season when you're alone. But if you stay open to letting others reach out to you, you may be surprised what happens.

SIMPLICITY MADE SIMPLE

The key to celebrating holidays without a family member or members of your family is to **PLAN AHEAD**. For example, if your child is going to be away over the holidays, talk to him or her beforehand and figure out when you can celebrate together. If you have recently lost a loved one, talk to friends and family about your feelings and how you want to celebrate well before the holiday descends on your head and heart.

Consider going solo. You never know. This could be a fantastic opportunity to take time out to indulge in a few of your favorite things. Or it may be the perfect time to do things you haven't had time for in the past such as visiting a museum, starting a new hobby, calling or writing old friends, or even reading a good book. Some experts suggest **MAKING A "SOLO PARTY EMERGENCY KIT"** filled with your favorite music and holiday treats.

Being far away from family and friends can make you feel sad or even hurt. Trying to hide your pain by overindulging in food or spending will only make things worse. Don't beat up on yourself about feeling down either. If you need to have a good cry, do it. Then make the decision to get on with the holiday. Don't be afraid to **SET YOUR OWN SCHEDULE**. If you feel as though you need some time alone, take it. If you feel the need for social engagements, then plan for them.

CREATE A SPECIAL CELEBRATION FOR THOSE WHO ARE AGED OR ILL and living in nursing homes. The holidays can be a time of stress for anyone, but if a loved one now resides in a nursing or caregiving facility it can be overwhelming for both the caregivers and the loved one. Many holiday celebrations simply provide too much stimulation and commotion for loved ones to deal with. Expecting them to join the family celebration can cause them to become disoriented and agitated. It is best to keep visits to smaller groups of people. If you bring them to your home, be sure to provide a quiet room where they can go if things get to be too hectic. Also, recognize that children's normal noise and movement are often very distracting and disconcerting to those with Alzheimer's disease, the elderly or the infirm. Television and other noisemakers also can be very stressful. Caregivers must not feel guilty about taking some time away so that they can relax and socialize. It's okay to enjoy a family event without your loved one present.

CELEBRATE SENSIBLY. My niece is the activities director for an assisted living facility. Here are some safe and fun activities that she recommends for celebrating with those who live in nursing homes and other residences: Drive around and see the holiday lights, visit the person's church or synagogue, bake cookies together, watch videos of past holiday celebrations, make tree decorations together, gather a group of strolling resident carolers and visit everyone in the facility.

Find new ways of celebrating with old traditions. Sometimes the best idea is to simply **ADAPT TRADITIONS** as a way of remembering a lost loved one through a special holiday ritual, such as crafting a decoration to hang on the tree.

GET INVOLVED IN HELPING OTHERS. I know several single folks who have made the holidays special for a lot of other people by committing themselves to selfless activities such as food drives, working at shelters or rescue missions, and visiting hospitals and nursing homes. I also read about one man who on Christmas morning decided to bake banana nut bread and take it around to all the neighbors whom he didn't know. It was the perfect way to make new friends and lift his spirit at the same time.

CELEBRATE WITH OTHER SINGLES. That's just what I did the first holiday after I was divorced. My single friends and I had a great time planning our celebration and inviting others who also needed a new "family by choice" to get together with.

Lord, somewhere in the great design of life, You decided that it is not good for me to be alone. Though I am often tempted to hide away, I will trust that You know what is best, and I will find someone with whom to celebrate this wonderful life You have given to me. Amen.

Holiday Blues

A man finds joy in giving an apt reply—
and how good is a timely word!

—PROVERBS 15:23 (NIV)

Depression is one of the leading causes of disability year-round, but you don't have to have a full-blown case of clinical depression to have the blues during the holiday season. Simply knowing what to say to someone suffering with holiday sadness can be difficult. We wish we could say the right thing at just the right time, but to do so requires a little knowledge and wisdom first.

For most of us, gathering with friends and family to celebrate, to reflect on the past and to dream about the future can be a happy and peaceful time. However, for some it can be a difficult time. The American Association for Geriatric Psychiatry (AAGP) says that older adults may feel more acutely the passing of time, the absence of parents, siblings and friends who have died, and the distance of loved ones who have moved away. Traditional reunions and rituals of the past may no longer be possible in their absence, leaving the holidays devoid of meaning.[12]

First, we must recognize that it is normal to feel reflective or even sad in the face of such losses of family and friends. The key is to notice when our senior loved ones continue to experience the "blues" long past the holidays. What seemed like a simple case of sadness may actually be a serious case of depression.

Contrary to popular belief, depression is not a natural part of aging. A person who is sad or anxious around the holidays will still be able to carry on with regular activities. When the holiday season ends, he or she should return to a normal mood state. However, AAGP says that when people continue to suffer with symptoms that interfere with their ability to function in everyday life, they may be clinically depressed. Depression is a medical illness and it should be evaluated and treated by a professional. When properly evaluated and treated, most people recover.

Your words can help lift the spirits of a loved senior who suffers from a simple case of holiday blues. First acknowledge that the holidays can be difficult for them. It's okay to admit that life is not always as cheery as the holiday advertisements make it appear. Discuss your own feelings about a time when you were feeling depressed or blue. It will help the person to know that you do understand how it feels. Encourage him to talk about any fond memories. The most important thing you can do is to simply listen.

LOOK FOR OTHERS WHO NEED ENCOURAGEMENT

The elderly aren't the only ones who can find the holidays more depressing than cheerful—children too can be affected. Depression runs in families, which means that some children are more vulnerable to depression than others. Dr. Ann Flynn, a psychiatrist who treats children and adolescents, says, "The holidays can make depression better, or they can make it worse, depending on the circumstances the child is in."[13]

For a child who has a positive relationship with his or her family members, the holidays will enhance that closeness. However, if the holidays are a reminder of what a child has lost through divorce or death of a parent, they can be more stressful. That makes it very important for the parent or caregiver to be sensitive to what the child is experiencing. The good news is that the holidays are also an opportunity to spend more time with a child. This will boost the child's self-esteem.

Depression in children does not look the same as it does in adults. Depressed children may act withdrawn but are also likely to engage in power struggles over the smallest things. They tend to pick fights at school and make self-deprecatory remarks. Challenging authority, falling grades and striking out at siblings are all signs of possible depression in children. Dr. Flynn's best advice is to simply use the holidays as an opportunity for intimacy by spending as much time together as possible. She also suggests creating holiday rituals. "Holidays have meaning, and they create symbols that children carry with them through adulthood," she said. "Rituals are important for children. So plan and take advantage of the opportunity for intimate activities."[14]

Sadly, anyone can become a victim of the holiday blues. The reality is that more people become depressed during the winter holiday season than at any other time. Lack of sunlight, the demands of shopping and preparation, financial limitations, high expectations, memories of loved ones who have died, and lack of sleep and rest all contribute to exacerbating our already overly busy lives. And sometimes, things get even worse immediately *after* the holidays. The fatigue, loneliness and disappointment over our unmet holiday expectations can be overwhelming.

As we learn to keep our expectations within reason for the season and plan for rest and relaxation, the holidays can be a catalyst for improving our mood. Living in the present, not comparing this year with some cloudy memory from the past, and simply enjoying those we love is a recipe for a holiday with a lot of heart as Guideposts writer Marilyn Morgan King found out:

> Every Christmas, after our family tree-trimming, we'd all stand back and admire our work, and then, without fail, someone would say, "It's the prettiest tree we've ever had!" Then we'd all laugh because those words had become a family ritual. In fact, each year the tree *did* seem prettier than ever before.
>
> But Christmas of 1988 was different. The children were grown, I was going through a divorce, and our daughter Karen was hospitalized three hundred miles from home. Our oldest son Paul and his family couldn't make it home for the holidays, so my son John, age twenty, and I went to Topeka, Kansas, to be with Karen. It was a somber trip. After attending Christmas Eve services at the hospital, we brought Karen to our motel room where we had a scrawny artificial tree two feet high with a few packages under it. It was a bleak setting, and the only prayer in my heart was, "Please, Lord, just get us through this." I'm sure Karen and John felt the same cold ache.
>
> But then came the moment of grace. John plugged in the little tree, turned off the overhead light and with a sweeping gesture and twinkle in his eye said, "May I present—*da, da da, DA*—the prettiest tree we've ever had!" Suddenly all three

of us were laughing and hugging, and hugging and laughing. We were still a family!

And that's how it came to pass that on a bleak December night in the year nineteen hundred and eighty-eight, in a small motel room in Topeka, Kansas, by the light of a scrawny artificial tree, there *was* room for Christ to be born in the inn. And by His grace, our family was held together in love.

SIMPLICITY MADE SIMPLE

KEEP THE HOLIDAYS POSITIVE. If you are an adult who fights depressed feelings during the holidays, do your best to keep your particular holiday demons at bay. This is especially important if you also happen to be a parent of a child at risk for depression. If parents allow themselves to be affected negatively by the holidays, children will pick up on this. Dr. Kenneth Johnson, a psychiatrist at Columbia St. Mary's, suggests defining for yourself what the holiday means for you and how you plan to make it a good memory. He says, "There's nothing magical about the holidays. If you don't get along with your sister during the year, you're not going to get along with her during the holidays." Understand that simple truth before you arrive for the big family gathering instead of setting yourself up for unrealistic expectations.[15]

Add a little light to your holidays. Those with a case of the wintertime blues may **FIND SOME RELIEF WITH LIGHT THERAPY**, which is also called phototherapy. You should first consult with your doctor, but most experts recommend ten thousand lux units, which translates into spending thirty to sixty minutes sitting under the light first thing in the morning. A full spectrum light box is the most common form of light therapy for Seasonal Affective Disorder (or SAD). There are many different lamp styles available for purchase from retailers. Simply ask for a ten thousand lux unit and then choose the one that most appropriately fits your needs.

KNOW THE WARNING SIGNS OF DEPRESSION. If your holiday blues last beyond two weeks and include crying spells, sleep problems, feelings of guilt or thoughts of death, you should seek medical care promptly. Other symptoms include withdrawal from regular social activities, lack of energy, excessive worrying, inability to concentrate and weight changes. If you or someone you know is displaying such symptoms, suggest that he or she visit the family doctor or a mental health practitioner. Remember that particularly for older folks, there may be a stigma attached to asking for help with depression or mental illness. Let the affected individual know that depression is treatable and something that one doesn't have to live with—whether one is thirty, sixty or ninety.

Be sensitive to children. **A CHILD WHO IS DEPRESSED NEEDS SPECIAL CONSIDERATION** regarding his or her schedule. Make necessary accommodations to keep a child as close as possible to the schedule she is accustomed to. Children, in general, need structure, consistency and attention—especially attention that does not involve toys or other material goods.

GET ANOTHER PERSPECTIVE. Sometimes, we simply need to express our feelings and concerns about the holidays. Take the time to talk things out with a friend or family member. An outside perspective might reveal more options than we can see by ourselves.

Father, teach me to recognize the signs of those
who need reminders of Your love. I know that in lifting
others, I, too, will be in a higher place. Amen.

Reindeers and Rudeness

A gentle answer turns away wrath,

but a harsh word stirs up anger.

—PROVERBS 15:1 (NIV)

Most of us would agree that it is better to respond to someone's anger with gentleness. Yet, despite the simplicity of this proverb, we all can become the victim or the cause of rude remarks during reindeer season—the holidays. Even Rudolph had to keep his spirit of Christmas despite the rudeness of his peers. Good manners should matter year-round. But during the holidays, we have an even greater expectation for the "spirit of Christmas" to invade our souls and make us gentle, patient and kind. However, the mere fact that we are attempting to fit in the joys of the season with the duties of parenting, shopping, decorating, entertaining, cooking and cleaning along with all our normal daily responsibilities sets us up for irritation.

A survey conducted by Public Agenda, called "Aggravating Circumstances— A Status Report on Rudeness in America, 2002," found that eight in ten people claim that lack of respect and courtesy is a serious problem. Six in ten say that in the past few years, rude behavior between strangers has become worse. In fact, forty-one percent of people admitted to being rude themselves.[16] Whether it is a minor slight by a sales clerk or a serious case of road rage, clearly many of us are intensely frustrated by the lack of respect we encounter in our daily lives—and it is worse during the holidays.

The average retail store is prime territory for this uncivil attitude. Three quarters of those surveyed said they have seen customers treat sales staff rudely. As many as sixty-four percent of those surveyed admitted to actually leaving a store because of the way sales staff treated them. It's no surprise that nearly all of us (ninety-four percent) are frustrated with the new communications technology—calling a company and getting a recording instead of a human!

P. M. Forni, cofounder of the Johns Hopkins Civility Project and author of *Choosing Civility*, says, "It will be largely up to *our* manners making our holidays more joyful than stressful for ourselves and others." Personal responsibility, *hmmm* . . . why is something that is so important so hard to find?

IT'S BETTER TO GIVE THAN TO RECEIVE

It's true that it is often *the other guy* who is rude. But Sandra Morisset, a professional etiquette trainer in New York City, says, "It's all about self-awareness and treating others with respect. If you're not aware of your behavior, that's a problem."[17] Most Americans rate their own manners as quite excellent, but the problem is that rudeness is on the rise. There has been a fifty percent jump in rudeness in only one year (2001–2002). This means that whether we are willing to own up to it or not, some of these rude people must include us!

For most of us, the holidays involve traveling. Take it from me, as someone who travels a lot, I know that there is no time when travel is not stressful. It can be a nightmare during the holidays. Amy Ziff, editor-at-large for Travelocity, says, "It's important that we all take time to examine our own actions to see if there are things we can do to help modify or eliminate rude behavior on the road." One study showed that the most festive and celebrated season of the year brings out some of the most not-so-merry behavior—especially among travelers.

More than half the survey respondents agreed that fellow travelers and drivers seemed ruder during the holiday season than at any other time. Fortunately, there are a few remedies to help travelers. First, be sure to know the rules at airports of what can be included in carry-on bags ahead of time so you can move through security quickly and easily. Since sixty-five percent of people cited waiting in long lines and losing one's patience as the most common trigger for rude behavior, plan to arrive at the airport during an off hour—even if it means being a few hours early for your flight. I often plan to arrive early at the airport and have a meal after checking in my baggage. I have found mid-morning and mid-afternoon to be the most convenient times of day at the airport.

But why do we behave so badly? There are probably dozens of reasons. Cynthia Gorsso, founder of the Charleston School of Protocol and Etiquette in South Carolina, cautions against pointing the finger at any one person or cause. She says, "We all find people irritating; that's a fact. But the bottom line is, how you treat people is not about how they are, it's about how you are."[18] And that takes us back to Proverbs 15:1: "A gentle answer turns away wrath, but a harsh word stirs up anger." It's as simple as loving others the way God loves us—warts and all—as Guideposts writer Phyllis Hobe realized one Christmas season:

Years ago when my husband and I were traveling through the western part of North Carolina, I bought a small wooden manger scene that had been made by someone living in the area. It has become my favorite Christmas ornament because it is so simple and so lovingly carved. Over the years, some of its more delicate parts have been broken and mended, but there it stands today, under my tree. It means even more to me now.

In many ways each one of us is very much like that little carving. We are made of simple material, but lovingly crafted by our Creator. There are no two of us exactly alike. We are not perfect; we haven't always held up well under life's pressures, but we have always been tenderly mended by a caring God. Even today, *especially* today, God looks upon us with deep love.

What can we give to God in return? Nothing. Christmas means that we can't give anything to God. It is He Who gives to us—His love, His care, His concern for our well-being, our struggles, our failures and our victories.

But Christmas also means that we can give to one another—not things, exhaustion, short tempers or heroic achievements, but simply the kind of undemanding, tenderly caring love that God gives to us. This is the way each one of us can truly bring joy to the world.

SIMPLICITY MADE SIMPLE

BE PATIENT. This is especially important when shopping. Everyone wants—and demands—attention, and the stores are almost always shorthanded.

Always say "please" and "thank you." Avoid using your cell phone in public. If you must, go to a restroom or lounge area to avoid interrupting other customers. Even among cell phone users, there are many who think that other Americans use their cell phones in a "somewhat" or "very" discourteous manner.

BE A SAFE, COURTEOUS AND CALM DRIVER. Americans find rude and dangerous drivers to be number three on their list of uncivil actions—and holiday traffic is worse than any other time of the year. The simple way to avoid getting tangled in such a discourteous situation is to not offend other drivers. The Dane County Sheriff's Office in Madison, Wisconsin, offered these suggestions: Don't cut off others. When you merge, make sure you have plenty of room. Use your turn signal. If you make a mistake and accidentally cut off someone, try to apologize with an appropriate gesture. Don't drive slowly in the left lane. If you are in the left lane and someone wants to pass, move over and let them by. You may be "in the right" but you may also be putting yourself in danger by angering drivers behind you. It is not your job to keep them from speeding. Don't tailgate. Drivers get angry when you do this. Allow at least a two-car-length space between your car and the car ahead of you. Be cautious and courteous and only rarely use your horn. If another driver seems eager to get in front of you, say "Be my guest." When you respond this way, after a while, "be my guest" becomes your automatic remark and you won't be as offended by other drivers' rudeness. Give angry drivers a lot of room. If another driver tries to pick a fight, put as much distance as possible between your car and his. *Do not*, under any circumstances, pull off to the side of the road and try to "settle things." Get help. If you believe the other driver is following you or trying to start a fight, either use your cell phone to call police or drive to a place where there are lots of people around. Then use your horn to get someone's attention.

GIVE KIDS A BREAK. Accept the fact that most children simply act their age. The problem is that we expect them to act like little adults when the reality is that they cannot. Christmas is just another day for children less than a year old. Toddlers, although lovable and cute, are curious. They are also demanding and exasperating. The best advice in anticipation of a young Christmas visitor is to childproof your home and don't try to make too much of Christmas until next year. Two-year-olds will be very excited about everything, but they care more about what glitters and shines than what awaits them inside boxes. It is also typical that two-year-olds don't share well. They are normally stubborn and don't necessarily like to shop. Three-year-olds want to be involved. Let them help decorate and wrap packages. Four-year-olds are simply silly, eager and fun. They love the holidays. The only problem is that they have more energy than any three adults. So be prepared to eat your Wheaties or Granola. Five-year-olds will actually enjoy sitting on Santa's lap and will also be happy to help keep Grandma's gift a secret. They love secrets!

BE A GOOD GUEST. Always RSVP, arrive on time, and call if you are going to be late. Don't bring a surprise guest! Bringing a giving attitude and your good cheer will contribute to the joy of the season. If you have been invited to be a houseguest, be sure to bring an appropriate gift. Offer to do chores such as washing dishes, while keeping your room and bathroom tidy. Keep children from being too noisy or disruptive. If you are hosting the party, be sure to find out in advance if anyone has any special dietary needs. At family gatherings, avoid topics that you know will set someone off. Also, do not boast about your big raise or talk about how badly you are doing financially. Also, don't bad-mouth any family members who are not present or embarrass family members who are. And no matter how tempting, *do not* go on and on about how amazing your children's or grandchildren's talents or accomplishments are.

Lord, I realize that I could be viewed as rude even when I'm not aware of it, but too often I simply lose control and offend others. Please forgive me for this selfish approach to holidays, and keep me from putting my own desires first. I pray to forgive others as You have forgiven me. Amen.

PART THREE

Deck the Halls with Happiness

CHRISTMAS IS A WONDERFUL TIME to celebrate with glitter and self-expression, when we can demonstrate our God-given creativity. Our personal style is reflected in the way we decorate and the gifts we present. In this section, I will give you suggestions and ideas on how to use simple household items to create a festive centerpiece, and show you how staying true to your own personal style makes the most memorable Christmas parties. Although Christmas is the perfect time to use our best china and most ambitious recipes, it is also a time to simply highlight what we love about others. Fill your house with music and people, and create time for baking together or making crafts. The gift of your time is one that nurtures both the giver and the receiver. Good memories will return to you throughout the coming years.

Christmas Creativity

So God created man in his own image,

in the image of God he created him. . . .

—GENESIS 1:27 (NIV)

I love knowing that we have been made in the image of the Creator. That means that we humans are different from the animals and all other creation. The fact that man and woman were made in God's image means we share a likeness with the most creative Being ever.

No matter who you are, you have the ability to be creative simply because you are an heir to the God who created all. You have inherited the ability to be creative. Even if you don't think of yourself as a creative person, you have the capacity to learn, to experiment and to create original expressions of your own ideas. And that is good news when it comes to getting ready for the holidays—especially Christmas, with all its potential adornment.

I have found that most people who *think* they are creative do express themselves artistically. Those who think they are *not* creative simply write themselves off as hopeless and don't even make an attempt. A few years ago, I was working with the *Later Today Show* on NBC. Jodie Applegate was one of the hosts, but she and I hardly ever got to work together because no one thought of her as "creative." Finally, one day they let Jodie do a decorating segment with me in which we used multiple layers of stencils to create a mural on a wall. As Jodie patiently and thoughtfully followed my direction, I could tell she was really enjoying the process. We all held our breath when it came time to remove her stencil pattern and reveal her work. The results were amazing! Jodie had painted an absolutely beautiful little pear on a pear tree with perfectly shaded leaves. She was thrilled as she said, "See, I can be creative!" I think all of us can be creative. It's simply a matter of practice and perseverance.

There is nothing like a handmade effort when it comes to creating a beautiful Christmas for your family; but don't let your lack of confidence hold you back. Whether it's wrapping presents with care, baking cookies or crafting a special gift, your efforts will be appreciated. The key—regardless of your talents and ability—is not to take on a bigger project than you actually have time for.

The whole point of creativity is to enjoy the process and not just the results. If you hate the process, you will never be able to appreciate the final work. Instead, every time you see it you will be reminded about what an awful time you had doing it. I read a quote once that said the pleasure derived from the process of whatever we do should be as great, if not greater, than the finished product.

I remember many, many years ago when I was first learning to knit that I had this not-so-brilliant idea to make as my first project a pair of white knee-high socks. As I struggled to get the stitches even, I found myself spending more time tearing out than knitting. The result was that one-third of the way through the first sock, the yarn was so dirty and raveled that it was pitiful. I hated that sock. If I had been forced to stick it out with that sock, I would never have knitted another thing in my life. The good news is that my mother realized my frustration and suggested another project. This kept me knitting. Now, all of my nieces and nephews have been blessed with many uniquely designed, hand-knit sweaters simply because I was steered by my mother in a direction that helped me enjoy the process.

Developing creative thinking can be as simple as practicing the process persistently. Even the most gifted artists study their craft. They also do several "rough" renditions of their paintings before actually beginning on a new piece of canvas. That's why many old masters' paintings continue to be found. They often are discovered on canvases that have been painted over as the artist practiced for a new painting. Creativity for us mere mortals is never effortless. Strong motivation is what gives us the energy necessary to generate original ideas.

EXPLORE YOUR CURIOSITY

The first rule of creativity is simply to be open to possibility. The fact is that most people are far more creative than they give themselves credit for. Johann Wolfgang von Goethe (1749–1832), the German poet, novelist, playwright, philosopher and one of the greatest figures in Western literature, was quoted as saying that if children were allowed to develop naturally from the day of their birth, they would all be pure geniuses.

What all creative processes have in common is tremendous curiosity. Curiosity leads us to being open to truly experiencing the world in all its beauty.

Dr. Gregory Benford, an astrophysicist at the University of California at Irvine, has written more than thirty books of science fiction, and he says the simplest way to get your creative juices flowing is to start with analogical thinking. He instructs his students to ask, "How is this thing like that thing, and how is it not?" He says we need to look for comparisons where we wouldn't ordinarily think there was any basis for similarity and go on from there to see if some new idea "comes out of the woodwork." He says creativity is really just a process of trying to make a connection that you didn't see before—but you have to be open to it.

Making a connection that she didn't see before is just what Guideposts writer Penney Schwab did one Christmas:

> "Did you put up the tree?" my sister Amanda asked when we visited by telephone the week before Christmas.
>
> "Don did. And, yes, it's a six-footer." My husband Don and I have argued over the tree size for thirty-eight years, the length of our marriage. Our family can tell by the size who chose the tree. "My other decorations are up too, such as they are. I envy those talented people who carry out a Christmas theme!"
>
> "I have a theme," Amanda said. "It's called 'Early Attic.'"
>
> "Since I don't have an attic, I guess my theme is 'Terribly Tacky,'" I responded.
>
> Later, I walked around the house and studied the decorations. The Nativity on the piano was made from cornshucks, not porcelain, but it reminded me of the stable and the humble surroundings of Christ's birth. The cut-tin candleholder

came from our church bazaar and shone as brightly as the star over Bethlehem. And the ornate stick-on window Nativity (number seven in a magazine list of "Ten Trashiest Decorations") had stunning colors that brought to mind the rich gifts of the wise men.

Then there was the tree, which even at six feet could barely contain all the ornaments. We bought the treetop star the Christmas after we married. We were in North Carolina, miles from friends and family. Michael and Rebecca's Sunday-school craft projects adorned the lower branches. Halfway up was the plaster-of-paris bell Patrick made in kindergarten; it hung right above paper decorations made by his three sons.

I didn't need talent or creativity or more money. I didn't even need a theme, because I already had one: Jesus. The ornaments and decorations are merely reminders of Him and His love. I looked over my beautiful Christmas house one more time, then went to the telephone to call Amanda.

SIMPLICITY MADE SIMPLE

Give yourself a break. One of the primary mistakes people make when it comes to creative work is listening to their own voice of judgment. They tell themselves that the work they are doing is not good enough or not creative enough. Another mistake is assuming that there is a right and wrong way to be creative. Just as each of us is unique, so too is the creative process. Creativity is variable. Creativity gives you **THE FREEDOM TO DEVELOP YOUR OWN STYLE**—and that is what makes it so cherished.

EVALUATE YOUR HOLIDAY ATMOSPHERE. This is some of the best advice I ever heard: instead of waiting until next year to decide what you are going to do and how creative you want to be, do it just before you put away all of this year's holiday glitter. Take a look around your home and begin writing down your thoughts and feelings about your decorations, gift-wrapping and whatever comes to mind. Think about how you would like to create an atmosphere that reflects you and your family during the holidays. Write down your most significant memory from this year. How can you expand on it for next year? What can you do to help get you and your family into the spirit of the season next time around?

KEEP A JOURNAL. Journaling is a great way to reflect on what you liked about past and present holidays and as a guide for building a better one next time. It's also a great place to map out your holiday plan. Journaling will help you determine where you are willing to invest your energy.

Remember, **CREATIVITY HAS NO BOUNDARIES** except your imagination. Your imagination can be stirred by going through magazines, shopping malls, etc. You simply have to ask yourself what gives you pleasure and how you can apply it creatively to your life. For example, do you like to doodle, draw or make patterns? Is calligraphy or poetry your favorite pastime? How about painting, decorating or growing flowers? Take some time to think about what you enjoy doing. Make a list arranged according to your preferences. Then set a goal to accomplish something beautiful with your own creative style.

GET ORGANIZED. Nothing stifles creativity faster than chaos. If you can't find what you need easily and quickly when you are in a creative mood, you will soon discover that you have lost the mood while hunting for your paintbrush!

Consider setting up a holiday organization center. One client of mine used an old dresser to store all her wrapping paper, ribbon, scissors, cards and other craft items. It made it simple for her to find time to create because everything she needed was in one place.

Father, as I behold the creative ways in which You impart good and perfect gifts to us, I am inspired to use creatively the talents You have given me. Please bless the work of my hands that I might reflect Your likeness as I decorate and make gifts for others this holiday season. Amen.

The Art of Holiday Décor

The holly's up, the house is all bright,

The tree is ready, The candles alight;

Rejoice and be glad, all children tonight!

—CARL AUGUST PETER CORNELIUS (1824–1874), "DER CHRISTBAUM"

Paging through each special edition magazine brimming with new ideas for holiday decorations can take your breath away. Yes, the pictures are dazzling—but interior design photos illustrating holiday décor can also be intimidating and make you feel overwhelmed. As you drag out the old boxes of mismatched and worn ornaments, don't be discouraged. There are a few simple steps to help add some strategic glitter to your holiday décor.

First, decide how much time, effort and money you are willing to spend decorating for the holidays. Most of us would agree the less the better, but we also want to be delighted by the beauty of Christmas. One reason for loving the season is that we get to spend more time with family and friends than we normally do. Finding just the right balance can be as simple as using decorating to encourage togetherness and establishing new traditions while creating special memories simply by doing some of the decorating together with family and friends.

Second, create a blueprint for your holiday decorations by deciding whether or not you want to use a theme. Lots of things can inspire a theme. For example, a favorite Scripture, poem or even a Christmas carol can be the inspiration for all your holiday décor. You can also be inspired by color. In fact, changing your holiday color can make a fabulous difference simply and inexpensively. Ribbons, a few new ornaments and natural plant materials can give an otherwise worn collection of decorations a completely different feel. And how it feels is what decorating is all about.

The whole point of decorating is to create an atmosphere that invites all to feel good about the season and to know that it is a special time. Theme decorating makes the entire process simpler because it allows you to focus and not be confused by so many options. As many who know me realize, my favorite place is the beach, so despite the fact that I live in a community far from the beach, I use shells as the theme for my holiday decorating scheme. The combination of shells, greens, lights and ribbon makes a festive appearance that announces Christmas in my own unique style without breaking the bank.

DO WHATEVER YOU CAN DO

Another way to simplify the holiday without diluting it is to choose to focus on doing just one thing exceptionally well. For many people a Christmas tree captures the best of all that the holiday is. Jo Robinson and Jean Coppock Staeheli, authors of *Unplug the Christmas Machine*, say that the way a tree looks is only part of how people feel about it. "Most people also respond to the sentimental value of familiar ornaments, whether or not they are beautiful. And they tend to get more enjoyment from a tree if they have had a good time decorating it. A tree decorated by one person spending a lot of time will often have a gratifying artistic unity to it, but a tree that involves the whole family is often more satisfying overall."

My friend, author Cris Bolley, reminded me that the reason we decorate is to help set the season apart from the other days—but sometimes, it just seems like too much effort. Here's how Cris got her Christmas groove back a few years ago:

In past years, my three daughters helped me decorate the house for Christmas. But as they have grown and moved on, decorating has become less eventful and simply more work for me. Last year, I had only one teenager left at home to decorate with me; but she was too busy to help me, and our nine-foot artificial tree was too heavy for me to handle alone. So I bought a four-foot, pre-lit tree for only twenty dollars and decorated it with all gold ornaments, cards and ribbons and set it in our front living-room window. I also used a fifty-percent-off coupon from the paper to buy an automated sleigh and reindeer to place in our front yard—again, it was something I could put up and plug in by myself since my husband was also losing interest in decorating the roofline with lights. It seemed to him that since the girls were grown, the purpose of decorating the house was losing its "pizzazz."

But once I put up the little tree and the dashing reindeer on the lawn, something amazing happened. Seeing my humble little effort to set the day apart, my teenage daughter insisted on getting the *big* tree out of the attic. Her boyfriend helped us put it together and we set it in the main entrance by the stairs. And on seeing my little sleigh and reindeer in the front yard, my husband was inspired to put lights on the shrubs and roof again. Soon all the mantles and countertops in the house were graced with pine boughs, lights and ornaments collected from years of merry Christmases.

When my nearly three-year-old granddaughter Riley came to visit us, Grammy's house was full of trees and exciting activity. When she was leaving the house that night she walked up to the reindeer on the lawn and stood motionless as she watched them leaping to take flight into the air. I watched her stand so still, as if afraid to scare them away. I stepped beside her as she stared at the wonder of the dancing deer against the backdrop of tiny lights on the house and trees. Quietly she whispered, "Grammy, can I ride them?"

The decorations had marked the day. . . . Christmas became a day when a little girl believed that anything might be possible. Without the lights and trees, Christmas would have been "just an ordinary day" at Grammy's house.

S I M P L I C I T Y M A D E S I M P L E

MAKE DECORATING THE TREE A SPECIAL FAMILY TRADITION. Start by assigning everyone a task and setting aside a whole day for the event. Be sure to reserve certain ornaments for each child to hang. Make the crowning star or angel a privilege for the youngest child to place on top of the tree (with a little help, of course). You could also make this a tree-trimming party and invite the neighbors or extended family. Be sure to set the mood with your favorite holiday music and eggnog. Encourage young children to make things to hang on the tree, and be sure to have the family collect ornaments year-round. I always shop for Christmas ornaments on vacation in the summer. Give your child or grandchild an ornament every year—eventually this can become a treasured collection that lasts a lifetime.

Master the art of tree lighting. David Stark, a Brooklyn floral designer, says the trick to hanging lights on your tree is to go up and down, not around. Start by dividing the tree vertically into three sections and string the lights by sections. Always plug in the lights *before* you begin to find those dastardly defective bulbs. Start at the bottom and weave each string in and out of the branches, to the top of the tree and back. David Murbach, manager of the Decorators for New York City's Rockefeller Center, says to **USE THE TRUNK-TO-TIP METHOD** to create "not just a shell of light but an inner glow and a three-dimensionality that cannot be achieved any other way."[19]

Indulge your senses. **INCORPORATING SIGHT, SOUND AND SMELL INTO YOUR HOLIDAY DÉCOR** will make your rooms most pleasing. Scents infuse and transform the season into a magical and unforgettable experience. The visual appeal of candlelight and the warmth it evokes have an undeniable appeal. The alluring aroma of spices and freshly baked goodies, the clean crisp scent of pine needles or the perfume of frankincense and myrrh are sure to put you in a holiday mood. Essential oils are an easy way to add holiday aroma. Homemade potpourri and sachets can be prepared five to six weeks ahead of the holiday season. In a plastic bag, sprinkle essential oil, dried flowers, leaves, nuts, seeds and berries. Or simply place a wreath of silk or dried florals and greens in a bag and scent with a few drops of your favorite essential oil. I love using juniper, cedar wood, spruce and balsam. You can also choose heady scents like myrrh and sandalwood. For spicy-scented tree ornaments combine 1 cup cinnamon, 1 tablespoon cloves, 1 tablespoon nutmeg, $^1/_2$ cup applesauce, 1 tablespoon sparkle stars and 2 tablespoons white glue. Once combined, roll out dough and cut with shaped cookie cutters (stars, snowmen, etc.). Use a straw to make a hole for the ribbon to hang. Dry for three to four days, turning regularly.

Go au naturel. **FRUIT MAKES THE PERFECT HOLIDAY ACCENT** in wreaths, garlands and centerpieces. Deck yours with cloves, ribbon, greenery, tassels and glitter. Real fruit works well for outdoor wreaths. Simply replace as needed. These wreaths can also last for several days indoors—adding a wonderful natural fragrance to your home. You can decorate with pears, apples, pineapple, pomegranates, berries, oranges, lemons, kumquats and sugar plums. To add some festive color to a plain white pillar candle, simply set it into a clear glass container, such as a bowl or even a hurricane globe, and add minilimes, rosy crab apples and some cranberries to create the perfect holiday blend. It's elegant, colorful and very easy to make. Wrap a pretty ribbon around the outside of the container and it's dressed for the season.

Avoid commercialism and **MAKE YOUR OWN HOLIDAY DECORATIONS**: styrofoam balls wrapped in ribbon make a pleasing mantle decoration. Use various sizes and colors and then add a little greenery to complete the look. Clear glass containers filled with holiday twinkle lights create the right atmosphere for adding sparkle to your holiday table or mantle. They can also be stuffed with treats such as candy canes, holiday gumdrops or even mints. Add a ribbon, flower or greenery and you have a beautiful and edible display for all!

> **Lord, thank You for making our smallest efforts seem grand in the eyes of those we love. Set loose creative ideas in me so that I will learn to use what I already have in order to bless people on Your behalf. Amen.**

Time for the Perfect Party!

Go, eat your food with gladness, and drink
your wine with a joyful heart, for it is now
that God favors what you do.

—ECCLESIASTES 9:7 (NIV)

A few years ago, I was scheduled to be the keynote speaker at a large conference. When I checked in the day before, just to make sure everything was
on schedule as planned, I was surprised to find out that somehow the conference
brochure had listed me as an "entertaining expert" instead of an interior
designer. That gave me exactly twenty-four hours to figure out what to do. As I
began thinking about how I entertain, I realized that there is a strong correlation
between decorating and entertaining. Just as I suggest that my design clients be
true to themselves and their lifestyle in their decorating—the same considera-
tions should be made for entertaining.

When decorating you must consider your family and way of living in a realistic setting—you can't expect to turn country bumpkins into fancy city slickers

simply by choosing formal furnishings. If you try, you will only find yourself disappointed. There is no rule that says just because it's Christmas, Thanksgiving or Easter that you must have a formal sit-down dinner. If you are really a chili person, then don't try to serve a seven-course fancy meal— serve chili out of a sparkling bucket and let everyone come in jeans and be comfortable.

My hypothesis was confirmed as I began researching this book. I found several books on entertaining written by interior designers. Each one of them came to the same conclusion that I did. It really can be as simple as asking yourself a couple of key questions whether you are considering decorating or entertaining: What are your family responsibilities and your lifestyle? How much time do you really have to devote to this project? How much money can you realistically afford to spend? What are your personality strengths and weaknesses? How many people can you, or do you expect to, entertain at once in your home? Ultimately, as the great American decorator Elsie De Wolfe extolled, the hallmarks of good taste are "simplicity and suitability."

When it comes to entertaining, it means choosing the right format for your home and your personality. If you have a small home, serve buffet style. If you have a small dining room or none at all, then set up tables in the living or family room. If you don't have fancy matching table linens, purchase some inexpensive fabric and drape it abundantly—allowing it to puddle on the floor—no sewing is required.

SIMPLY ENJOY YOURSELF AND YOUR GUESTS

Ultimately, your goal should be to make sure that you and your guests enjoy each other. Notice that I said *you* and your guests. Make it easy on yourself—

the more you enjoy yourself, the more your guests will enjoy themselves. A buffet dinner can be as grand as a formally seated multicourse meal. It's all in your attitude. Entertaining is an opportunity to express your ideas of what a party should be rather than following the dictates of any entertaining diva. Remember that this is the season to celebrate. That means it should be fun. Have fun planning your menu. Have fun making your home look and smell inviting. If pulling out your finest china and your best party dress makes you feel good—then do it—just as Guideposts writer Van Varner's family did:

"A tuxedo!" my brother boomed on the phone to me from Chicago. "Kit wants me to bring a tuxedo! I won't do it. I haven't worn that thing in years!"

I belong to a small family: one older brother Ham and his two married sons. Ham and I are always together at Christmas, either with my nephew in central Illinois, or with the other one in Tennessee. This was the Illinois year. I wondered what formal festivity Kit could have in mind.

"Nothing special," Kit said as I arrived and his two small kids swarmed over me in noisy welcome. "Iris and I just figured we'd like to dress for dinner on Christmas Eve. Family only."

My brother glared. He had that what-have-I-done-wrong expression on his face, that exasperated look of I-didn't-raise-my-son-to-put-on-airs-right-here-in-the-middle-of-these-Midwest-cornfields.

On Christmas Eve I dutifully put on my black tie, and when I came into the living room, Iris was quietly lighting candles, a picture of grace in a shimmering blue gown. Kit, in his tuxedo, was finishing with the logs for the fireplace. The children arrived: Katrin smiling, in love with the romance of her red velvet party dress; little Eric in dark blue serge and black bow tie, stoical, yet intrigued.

Then Ham came. He'd brought his formal clothes after all! Automatically, we all stood up. I'd never seen him more handsome, more patriarchal. He had a dignity that I hadn't bothered to find in him for years.

Dignity—that was the key word for our Christmas. No hubbub, no arguments, no loudness. We laughed and reminisced. The kids sat up straight at the table without being told. And after dinner, Ham looked across at his son and said, "It was a good idea, Kit-boy."

Was it the dinner clothes that made our Christmas? No, not the clothes. It was the disciplined effort we made to honor an occasion. I'm not sure all of us recognized it that evening, but we dressed to honor the birthday of Jesus Christ. And you see . . .

I have found: That paying respect when respect is due costs little, but its value cannot be calculated.

SIMPLICITY MADE SIMPLE

CREATE LASTING MEMORIES. A special party, like Van's family party, is unforgettable and will outlast any gifts exchanged that year. The basics for any party are the same—but it's how you customize the details that makes the difference. Think in terms of hospitality rather than making the social grade. Dress up your table with your favorite serving dishes. Use that heirloom silver and pretty porcelain you've been saving. If you don't have any—then invest in simple white platters. They can be found almost anywhere and are elegant and inexpensive. Measure your success by how heartily your guests eat, laugh and talk.

Serve comfort food. **SIMPLE CAN BE EXTRAVAGANT.** Start by deciding what kind of menu you want as far ahead as possible. Do you want to serve sitdown or buffet style? One of my favorite holiday meals is a standing rib roast served with my version of Yorkshire pudding. I make the pudding in muffin tins. It never fails and makes serving so much easier. Always include some healthy, low-calorie selections. Try serving something unusual when it comes to vegetables. My new mashed favorite is cauliflower. Serve it as you would mashed potatoes. Prepare and freeze whatever you can in advance. Don't feel as though you have to make everything from scratch. Order specialty items or even dessert from your favorite bakery. For a buffet style meal, avoid anything that can spoil when left out for hours.

Plan your table. I always set my table the day before. It's something my mother always did—so I guess it just stuck with me. I love dressing the table—it is one of the more relaxing things for me to do. A *tablescape*, kind of like a landscape, is a great way to **MAKE A TABLE SPECIAL.** It's also a fun way to make a unique statement and is enjoyable to plan. Consider combining the color(s) you used throughout the house for your napkins, tablecloth, placemats and centerpiece. I love to incorporate candles into my centerpiece as well as greenery, berries, fruits or shells. But use whatever appeals to you.

One year I used fresh vegetables and shined them with oil. Another year I used pebbles and candles. Allow yourself to simply have fun.

MAKE A MASTER LIST of what must be done one month, one week and one day in advance. Be sure to plan your seating arrangement too. This is especially helpful in keeping old family rivalries from being revived. Place talkers with nontalkers to keep the conversation lively. Be sure to inquire if anyone has any special dietary needs or food allergies. Choose recipes that are familiar and do not require you to spend a lot of time in the kitchen. Your guests will begin to feel guilty if you do. Do as much of your shopping as you can two weeks ahead—leaving only those things that cannot be done in advance for the day of or day before the party.

ENLIST HELP. A great way to make children feel important and ease your workload during the party is to enlist children to greet guests at the door, handle their coats, and also to introduce anyone new to the rest of the group. Be sure to assign a couple of children as official photographers. Then create a collage of photos along with a "thank you for coming" letter to send to all your guests. It's a great way to keep the holiday spirit. Remember, your guests should be the focus. The goal of a holiday party should be to put everyone in a festive mood to set the tone for the coming year.

> Lord, it seems that the years are remembered only by these special days that we set aside for each other. Thank You for giving us reason to celebrate, and for filling our tables with more than enough for everyone. Amen.

Warm, Fuzzy and Fun!

But Martha was distracted by all the preparations
that had to be made. She came to him and asked,
"Lord, don't you care that my sister has left me
to do the work by myself? Tell her to help me!"

—LUKE 10:40 (NIV)

It's amazing the difference an attitude can make. Holiday preparations can be a drag, or they can be a wonderful time for family fun and bonding. It's all in how you see it. When I think about all the Christmases past, it astonishes me how many of the best times were actually about preparing food that involved a lot of work. At Easter, every year, my family makes fresh kielbasa from scratch with Great-grandma's old sausage stuffer. Even the men get involved as they gently coax the skins open so that the women can fill them.

From as far back as I can remember, Mom baked cookies at Christmas. I don't mean a few dozen—I mean enough cookies to last two or three months for a family of eight! Mom has several old and very large lidded crocks. As the cookies cooled they were placed gently into the crocks for storing. The crocks of cookies were kept in our outer foyer—where it was as cold as a refrigerator—or colder, depending on the Cleveland winter. Baking cookies was something that we children were encouraged to participate in. Thumbprint cookies were always a favorite. After all, what could be more fun than sticking your pudgy little thumb into cookie dough! *Mmm, mmm,* good.

When I called my sister Wendy, who is ten years younger, and asked her what the most significant holiday activity is for her she responded without hesitation—"baking cookies!" And her favorite cookies are: "Thumbprints and Kolachi." Kolachi are a traditional Polish cookie that can be filled with almost any kind of fruit preserve. Today, our family holiday cookie-baking tradition continues and now includes grandchildren whose own children will soon be adding their chubby little thumbprints to the cookies.

WORKING TOGETHER BONDS US TOGETHER

A family here in Lancaster, Pennsylvania, has found crafts to be their holiday family-bonding time. Inch by inch, their family bonds grow stronger. There is a sense of family togetherness as the parents help their children, ages four and six, weave a pipe cleaner through felt to build wiggly inchworms. Crafts, from cross-stitch to homemade Christmas ornaments, help keep this family close. "Crafts are a pretty big thing in our home," says Mom. "It's time spent together. Not just staring at the TV and not saying anything—it's actually learning something and actually interacting. It also gives the children a sense of accomplishment," she says.

According to Terry Ouellete, a national spokeswoman for the nonprofit

Craft and Hobby Association, the number one reason people do crafts is to make gifts for someone. That makes crafting a nearly perfect holiday activity. It's a chance for family team-building and an opportunity to create one-of-a-kind gifts for those you love.

CHRISTMAS IS A TIME FOR SINGING

One of the oldest holiday activities is caroling. Caroling has a lively and varied history that started with the angels singing at Christ's birth. In Britain the carolers are called *waits* because they return on Boxing Day for their tips. They are traditionally pictured gathered around a lantern, but in many parts of Europe "star singers" take part in the job of singing from house to house. They carry a great star in memory of the Star of Bethlehem and sometimes they even dress up as Magi and other figures from the Nativity.

In Poland the cardboard star is made to revolve like a pinwheel and usually one of the boy carolers wears a goat mask. A goat figure was originally the personification of the devil. This figure also appears in Sweden, where the rest of the caroling star boys dress in white and act out short biblical scenes as they sing. In Romania a wooden star is adorned with frills, little bells and a manger scene. In Finland the carolers, usually boys, raise large sums of money for charity with a play about the Three Kings.

In Mexico and South America there is an abundance of dance and drama surrounding the carolers. Throughout Scandinavia the old medieval meaning of carolers as ring dancers has translated into families simply gathering in a circle around the tree on Christmas Eve to sing traditional songs. Today, caroling too often has translated into attending large organized concerts rather than actually strolling about outdoors and singing in city streets and neighborhoods. That's too bad, because the simplicity of caroling is one of the most inspiring activities you can do as Guideposts writer Phyllis Hobe discovered:

A few years ago some neighbors invited me to go caroling with them a few nights before Christmas. I didn't think I should because I had so much to do, but the idea appealed to me. Somehow I found the time, and I'm glad I did. Because on that windy, bitterly cold night, as we trudged from house to house, singing those beautiful carols, greeted by smiles of surprised delight, I felt the joy of Christmas. For a few hours, I was free to think of nothing but the coming of Christ to earth and all that means.

Joy is the ability to give to others the love God gives to us, something I'd forgotten in the midst of holiday distractions and the usual complaint, "so much to do, and so little time."

But on this night the true meaning of Christmas returned to me—I saw that Christ isn't Someone we have to find. He has already found us. We don't have to follow a star or wait on a lonely hillside for a sign of His arrival. He is here, not only on earth, but in our hearts and in our lives.

This year, will you join me in truly celebrating Christ's coming? Let Him be a part of everything we do, from our quiet moments to our hurried attempts to do more than we can. Let Him enable us to put His love into our efforts. Let us not look far . . . He is here.

SIMPLICITY MADE SIMPLE

Remember, it's the simple things that usually mean the most. Just as our family's fondest joy is baking lots and lots of cookies together, you too can find great joy in a simple activity as long as it involves the people you love. One idea that not only benefits those less fortunate than ourselves but also helps clean out the clutter is to take the time after opening your presents to **PUT TOGETHER A BASKET OF GOOD STUFF YOU NO LONGER NEED** to give to a charitable organization.

MAKE THINGS IN MULTIPLES. Big-batch baking or cooking is the perfect family holiday activity. Whether it's soup, stew or lemon pound cake, this is a great way to get some of the holiday preparations done while having a blast. Put on your favorite holiday music and sing while you work. One family of sisters watched their favorite holiday movie while baking and cooking. They laughed. They cried. They danced. They loved!

Recapture the holiday spirit simply by playing games with children. Their innocent sense of celebration is contagious. Allow yourself the freedom to act like a child. Laugh at yourself and **INVEST YOUR ENERGY IN SOMETHING TOTALLY PLAYFUL.** Try seeing the holiday through the eyes of a child. Look for the magic and the miraculous. Take time to relish the sounds, sensations, sights, tastes and smells of Christmas.

Reminisce. Bring out old photos that evoke happy times. It's a fine way to keep family history alive and relevant. You may even want to incorporate photos into your decorating. It's a great way to inspire a sense of importance to the family. **RECORD YOUR MEMORIES AND CREATE NEW TRADITIONS.** As your family gathers around the dinner table, use this time to make plans for next year. One idea could be to plan to offer a hand, together as a family, within your community. Ask everyone to volunteer ideas about where and how to help.

Honor those no longer with you by **USING OLD FAMILY TIME-HONORED RECIPES** as part of your celebration. Kolachi cookies have a long history in my family that goes back generations. But the "secret" recipe has been guarded and never shared with anyone who was not related to us. Even when my sister asked Mom if she could share it with a very good friend, Mom said no.

> **Jesus, loving You puts music in our hearts. Thank You for opportunities to sing Your praises in the marketplaces and in our homes through the holiday season while enjoying the abundant life You have granted to us. Amen.**

Holiday Self-Care

"This season is all about gifts. Gifts that
nurture the souls of both the giver and given.
Perfect gifts. The gifts of Spirit."

—SARAH BAN BREATHNACH, AUTHOR OF *SIMPLE ABUNDANCE*

Think about the kind of gift that you could give that would nurture your soul as well as the soul of the recipient. What would it look like, feel like? Perhaps the gift of learning how to receive graciously would be one gift that could nurture both the giver and the receiver. Think about how many times you have found yourself saying: "No thank you, I can do this myself," when someone offered to help you.

Just recently, I offered to do the dishes after having a home-cooked meal with an elderly couple who have trouble getting around. Despite her physical struggle, the lady of the house just could not allow me to do the dishes. Why? I don't know for sure, but I suspect that part of the reason is that she simply has her own way of doing things. Yesterday, my goddaughter Lex was telling me about how she helped a friend fold laundry this past week. Much to Lex's surprise, her friend refolded everything that she had helped her with. Lex said, "I don't know how her soon-to-be-husband is going to handle her need to have everything perfect!"

Author of *Life Makeovers*, personal coach and lecturer Cheryl Richardson says, "Receiving is an act of generosity! One of the greatest gifts we give to others is our willingness to let them give to us." She suggests that we need to learn to stop, take a deep breath and try something new like: "Yes, I'd love help with the dishes," and "Thank you for offering to make life easier."

FILL YOUR HOLIDAYS WITH SERENITY

Learning to master the art of laziness during the holidays may indeed be another recipe for a happy holiday. For example, why not give yourself permission to sleep an hour or two longer than you normally would? Or if you still struggle with letting others help you clean up after dinner, try letting the dishes sit on the table long after the holiday meal is over so you can simply enjoy talking with your guests rather than slaving in the kitchen. If you start cleaning up, you make your guests feel uncomfortable or worse. Soon they will feel so guilty that they will be compelled to clean with you instead of visiting with you. The whole point of inviting people to your home is to enjoy them! Of course if they cheerfully volunteer to help you, then make the best of both ideas and receive the offer for help gracefully, and combine the work in the kitchen with holiday stories or something that you all enjoy talking about.

Be selective with the activities that you have been invited to and choose only to attend those that you know will be a wonderful experience. My sister Lorie is very good at taking care of herself during the holidays by not allowing herself to become overwhelmed with too many parties. She knows that parties stress her out so she is careful about which invitations she accepts. She never hesitates to say that it would simply be too much for her. She knows her limitations and honors them. I give her a lot of credit for this. Protecting herself keeps her more relaxed. The more relaxed she is, the more loving her attitude is toward others. She prefers to be able to give the kinder, more loving part of herself to those she loves.

Often during the holidays, some of our self-care activities can be lost in all the hustle and bustle of the season. Yet taking the best care of ourselves during the holiday season can contribute greatly to overcoming the sensation of being overwhelmed. Amidst all the preparations, shopping, wrapping and celebrating, why not give the gift of pampering? Sharing this gift with your mother, sister or best friend by arranging for a massage, pedicure or simply a day at the movies can easily nurture both of you.

And some of the best gifts don't have to cost money. Try trading a massage or pedicure with each other. It's a simple and effective way of helping your body relax while investing in quality time together. In our fast-paced world, especially around the holidays, we drag our bodies around nonstop to the point of near exhaustion. To keep our energy up, we must practice extreme self-care.

As I urged in the beginning of this book, define clearly for yourself what seasonal experiences are important to you. If you don't know what you really want during the holidays, then it will be much harder to determine which invitations are or are not in alignment with your desires. By clearly pinpointing your preferences in writing, it gives you a place to start your evaluation. Remember also to share your desired holiday preferences with your spouse and other loved ones, asking them what their desires are too.

The secret to a happy holiday is learning to collaborate and to create a plan that is uniquely yours with a goal to experience more serenity, more joy and more opportunities to nurture the souls of those you love.

SIMPLICITY MADE SIMPLE

Make yourself a promise to take enough quality time for yourself. You deserve **TIME AWAY—ALONE.** This is not being selfish; it is simply a way to commune with yourself and God. If you don't take time to go to the well for water, you will not have what is essential to quench the thirst of your soul. A dry soul has no resource for nurturing others.

RECOGNIZE THAT YOU ARE NOT SUPERWOMAN. You cannot provide unlimited care for everyone. You have limits. Acknowledging those limits helps to reduce anxiety and improve the love you give. Be proactive in taking steps to lessen your stress.

Don't be embarrassed or ashamed to ask for help. Remember this is an opportunity to **PRACTICE THE ACT OF GENEROSITY RECEIVED** by letting others give the gift of helping. Be willing to share the care.

KEEP YOUR NUTRITION GOALS ON TRACK. Many things can make this challenging: extra social events, tempting treats or travel. The holidays in general interfere with our regular eating habits. Don't skip meals, especially not breakfast. If you do you will only be hungrier later and more likely to overindulge in unhealthy foods. Pace yourself when faced with tempting goodies and sweets. Seek out healthier food choices such as the fruit or veggie trays. To boost your much-needed energy, be sure to increase your carbs and protein. Cereal and milk, yogurt, cheese and crackers, peanut butter and pretzels are all good choices. Practice paying attention to when your body is hungry or comfortably full and respond accordingly. Try to put less focus on the food and more on enjoying conversation and other activities.

Choose how to spend your time wisely. **BUILD TIME INTO YOUR SCHEDULE TO RELAX** and enjoy the festive season. Give yourself the gift of extra time with loved ones who make you feel great. Stay in touch with a friend who's easily accessible for venting. My friend Jan and I have a mutual pact that whenever one of us needs to vent, we make ourselves available. Sometimes it's just a few emergency minutes in the driveway for debriefing our anxiety. You might even consider scheduling time for just such an occasion.

DO WHAT MAKES YOU SMILE. If running outside to make snow angels with your children or grandchildren is something you love to do, then do it. If taking a long hot bath in the middle of the day with your favorite bath scent, candles and music makes you feel good, do it. Take time for yourself each day to slow down and calm your body, mind and spirit. You will need this time more than ever during the holidays to maintain a healthy lifestyle—and frame of mind. Worship with family and friends. This will lift you above the countless holiday details and allow you to focus on God and others. Celebrate the things that are truly important—family, friends, giving and, most of all, love. Do something for your health, something for your heart and something for your soul. I promise that your holiday stress will drop and your joy will increase abundantly.

Lord, I will give wisely this holiday, looking for ways to nurture the ones that I love with gifts that strengthen them. I will also look for ways to set good examples for those in my realm of influence so they see that Your goodness and mercy keep me in perfect peace. Amen.

PART FOUR

The Perfect Gift

GIFT-GIVING is a huge part of the holidays, but it is easy to confuse a gift or its cost with the love and concern we really wish to express. Gifts don't have to always be something we buy. They can be something we make or even do for someone. Let's talk, then, about creating lists, checking them twice and making a budget of both time and money so that we can truly enjoy the art of giving to others. Real joy in gift-giving comes from taking time to know people so well that we can give something to them that reflects our appreciation of who they are. The best gifts make a person feel esteemed, rather than in need of charity. That kind of gift can only come from spending time with people—in other words, giving of ourselves is the greatest gift we can offer to anyone.

The Gift of Giving

When they saw the star, they rejoiced exceedingly with
great joy. And they came into the house and saw the Child
with Mary His mother; and they fell down and worshiped
Him; and opening their treasures, they presented to Him
gifts of gold and frankincense and myrrh.

—MATTHEW 2:10–11 (NAS)

The ancient tradition of gift-giving is filled with the desire to express our generosity, compassion and love to those we cherish. As we remember the simple birth of our Savior, we give thanks for the miracle of His life. And perhaps in a way our gift-giving is a response to His great gift to all of us. There is hope in each gift given that it will also renew the miracle and the wonder of Christ's life and death and the impact it has had on our lives.

The gifts the Magi brought to the Christ Child were of royal quality. Frankincense was a fragrance important in establishing the proper atmosphere for worship; myrrh was a precious substance used for embalming; and gold continues to be unrivaled for its monetary significance. These gifts all had value and were a testament to the significance of this baby's divine mission.

It has been two millennia since the Magi carried gifts to celebrate Christ's birth. But when we think about gift-giving today, it's disappointing to see how we sometimes give out of habit rather than for the purpose of celebrating Christ's presence in our lives. Nancy Loving Tubesing and Donald A. Tubesing, authors of *Kicking Your Holiday Stress Habits*, described our situation this way, "The child in each of us is fascinated with the giving/receiving aspect of the holidays. We are greedy. We are afraid we won't get what we want. We want everything and can't set priorities. We give away what we wish to receive. We try to please others with our gifts. We confuse the gift or the cost of the gift with the love and concern we really wish to give or receive. It's the Santa Claus trap."[20] Sadly, the trap was set some time ago.

Will Rogers was quoted as saying, "The whole Christmas thing started in a fine spirit. It was to give happiness to the young, and another holiday to the old, so it was relished by practically everybody. It was a great day, the presents were inexpensive and received with much joy and gratification. . . . The merest little toy was a boon to their young lives, and what a kick it was to the parents to have them rush back up to the bedroom to show you 'what Santa brought.'"

So where do we go from here? Let's start with examining why we give gifts at all. Cynthia Yates, author of *The Complete Guide to Creative Gift-Giving*, says, "We give to honor others, whether for personal accomplishment, life passage, or simply because of feelings of friendship and love. Our best gifts bear tidings of goodwill, of kindness, of praise, or respect. We give because we *want* to give."[21] Just as the Magi honored the Christ Child, do we wish to honor those we love. That's why it's so important to us to find *exactly* the right gift.

But that is precisely what causes us to get caught in the Santa Claus trap. Our motivation and desires are good. Our timing, budget and planning are usually not. So when we find ourselves up against the clock, we run to the mall and buy something expensive, faddish, silly or inappropriate. The fact is that locating meaningful gifts takes time and planning—including financial planning. The good news is that there are some simple and effective ideas to help you avoid repeating these mistakes.

THE SECRET TO GIVING CHERISHED GIFTS

First, we need to recognize that not all gifts come with a price tag. Yates says in her book, "Kindness, compassion, unconditional love, and selfless sharing do not need big red bows or Christmas tree tinsel." Secondly, as the adage says, it's the thought that counts. We need to remember this as we contemplate the perfect gift.

One of my most cherished gifts is a simple red step stool that came from my hubby, Dave. It sits cheerfully in my kitchen waiting to be used, which is often, because I am very petite. I absolutely needed those extra steps. The color makes me happy, but it's the fact that Dave realized my dilemma and found a creative way to solve it that matters most, especially coming from a nearly six-foot-five-inch-tall man! His personal attention to my needs makes me feel loved. And love is just what Guideposts writer Patricia Houck Sprinkle discovered to be the secret of great gift-giving:

> Three-year-old Barnabas, two-month-old David and I were traveling alone at Christmas. As we left the plane, a helpful stewardess said, "I think I'll take that cute baby home with me."
> Barnabas stared up at her in horror. "You can't! He's *our*

baby, and very precious to us!" I have treasured that remark through the many brotherly battles over the years.

I also think of it at Christmas and realize, in a small way, just what it was that God *gave*. What would it take for me to send one of my precious sons to a faraway land to grow up among strangers, suffer their scorn and die from their hostility?

God gave a precious Gift out of an incredible love.

That's what Christmas is all about.

Thinking of what God gave can help me choose appropriate Christmas gifts for others. My choice is not between a book and a record or between a gift that's too extravagant and one that's cheap. My choice is between a gift that says, "Here's a present" and a carefully chosen one that says, "I love you."

SIMPLICITY MADE SIMPLE

JUST LIKE SANTA—MAKE A LIST! Many experts agree that the simplest way to be prepared for gift-giving is to make a list of all the people and events over the next year for which you will need a gift. Take into consideration possible weddings, anniversaries, engagements, holidays and birthdays, anything that might require a gift. Cynthia Yates suggests even including people to whom you will be giving no-cost gifts, like the elderly man down the street who would probably appreciate a gift of laughter and good conversation or good listening. Once the list is established begin to brainstorm gift ideas and assign a possible cost for each. Study this carefully. It will become your guide and tool for shopping.

CREATE A MONTHLY GIFT BUDGET. By simply adding a specific amount of money to your regular budget, you will resist the temptation to charge more than you can afford. It will also make it easier to pare down your gift-giving where you can and keep focused on finding new and creative ways to give no-cost gifts.

KEEP AN EYE OUT FOR SALES and unexpected finds! With your gift list in hand—you can easily take advantage of after-Christmas sales and other seasonal sales throughout the year. Find a corner or a closet to stash your treasures until you need them. But always, always check this stash frequently so that you will not forget to give a prepurchased gift—as I did. My husband received last Christmas's gift of pajamas early this spring. They had been completely forgotten in the gift closet! Now I mark my calendar after purchasing a gift for a certain event. For example, I have already purchased my goddaughter's birthday gift for September—so I have made a note on her birth date that the gift is in the closet.

REFINE YOUR LIST. My family is large and continues to grow. We solved the overspending and overgifting problem by agreeing that only children under age twenty-one would receive gifts. When my nieces and nephews were young, they received their gifts from their godparent(s). Now that they are grown with children of their own, the tradition continues to the next generation. Remember that the holidays will quickly lose their luster when the material gift-giving becomes the all-encompassing focus of the occasion.

DON'T LET GIFT-GIVING MYTHS FOUL YOU UP. You are not obligated to reciprocate just because someone gave you a gift. When this happens, simply accept the gift graciously. Another myth is thinking that there should be equality in gift-giving. If someone gives you an expensive gift, you don't have to feel bad for giving something less expensive. Most likely, your friend and family already know your financial situation and wouldn't want you to spend more than you could comfortably afford.

Lord, forgive me for seasons past when I have given to others out of obligation rather than a cheerful heart. From this day forward, help me to focus on the value of those who receive my gifts rather than the expense of the gift. Amen.

Become a Gift

Rings and jewels are not gifts, but apologies for gifts.

The only gift is a portion of thyself.

—RALPH WALDO EMERSON (1803–1882)
"GIFTS" FROM *ESSAYS: SECOND SERIES*

E merson continues, "Therefore the poet brings his poem; the shepherd, his lamb; the farmer, corn; the miner, a gem; the sailor, coral and shells; the painter, his picture; the girl, a handkerchief of her own sewing. This is right and pleasing, for it restores society in so far to its primary basis, when a man's biography is conveyed in his gift, and every man's wealth is an index of his merit. But it is a cold, lifeless business when you go to the shops to buy me something, which does not represent your life and talent, but a goldsmith's" (*Essays: Second Series*).

By Emerson's standard the best possible and most appropriate gift might just be the gift of yourself or your talent. But how do you become a gift? The simplest answer is to give the gift of time. How many times have you said, "There just aren't enough hours in the day"? Even if you don't say it, you probably think it almost every day. The simple fact is that most people are chronically busy, which makes the gift of time a most valuable commodity. Nancy Twigg, author of *Celebrate Simply*, says, "Many people would much rather give up some of their money than to sacrifice a portion of their precious free time. Unlike store-bought presents, gifts of time are not duplicable." And for those who have more time than money, it's a simple way to show you care without overspending.

GIVE WHAT NO ONE ELSE CAN

Free gifts can be some of the most expensive gifts to give because they require personal sacrifice, time and effort. It would certainly be easier to simply buy and give a present. But it is worth the effort because the receiver will recognize the value of your sacrifice and appreciate your willingness to give of yourself. Therefore, let your giving be inspired. Kristin M. Tucker and Rebecca Lowe Warren, authors of *Celebrate the Wonder: A Family Christmas Treasury*, say, "There are hundreds of ways to become a gift. Enjoying a concert with a friend, teaching a neighbor to fish, baby-sitting for a relative . . . Sharing yourself with those on your gift list is a wonderful celebration of the spirit of Christmas." Something as simple as the gift of a compliment, a telephone call or a word of encouragement is one possible way to give every day.

A few years ago, while my grandmother Irene was still alive, I had the opportunity to travel for business twice a month to California to where she lived. I made sure to rent a car and stay a few days extra each time so I could visit with her. Those were some of the best and sweetest times of my life. Sometimes, we sat and chatted or walked along the beach. Other times we went shopping—Grandma never owned or drove a car—so the opportunity to go far beyond the bus line was particularly exciting despite the fact that Grandma never spent much money. It was simply the pleasure of being together. But the best part was when I would return home and unpack my suitcase. I always found a love note and a small token gift. Sometimes it was something that she loved and wanted me to have and other times it would be something as simple as a small bottle of hand lotion. I cherished them all.

The heart of the matter is to mix your creative juices with loving care to create a gift without measure, just as Guideposts writer Samantha McGarrity did:

> There was absolutely no money for Christmas gifts. And so many people to remember! I racked my brain to find a way to show my love for those who meant so much to me.
>
> Thinking back to memorable gifts, I remembered how Grandmother, now ninety-five, always used to give me something that had belonged to her, something she had treasured and enjoyed through the years and then passed on to me to enjoy. *Those* gifts were the most prized!
>
> And so I looked about me, and discovered "gifts" among my possessions—a book of Longfellow's poems for Tim, a wind chime for Mother, cloisonné barrettes for Hillary, and so on down my list of family and friends. These gifts had been a part of my home for years, and all had given me some special joy. Now, giving them to people I loved helped me share that joy.
>
> I felt thankful for a grandmother who taught me how to truly give—with gifts from the heart.

SIMPLICITY MADE SIMPLE

There are lots of **FREE OR ALMOST FREE GIFTS** that are simple and meaningful. For example, an IOU for something that usually costs money such as painting a room, babysitting, mowing grass, even grocery shopping can mean a lot. Be creative. When my friend Jan and her husband were just married and struggling financially, they took a lot of photos of their parents throughout the year. From the photos they made a decorative collage for every member of the family. Those gifts were among the most treasured for years. If you can draw, write, paint or craft, create a piece of art in honor of a loved one.

Give a busy mom some peace and quiet. Perhaps you know someone who could use an afternoon alone. It might be your spouse, daughter or a parent. Give the person a coupon entitling him or her to two hours of peace and quiet while you take the kids for an afternoon. It doesn't even have to be a young person with children. Caretakers really appreciate and need an afternoon off. **A GIFT OF YOUR TIME** to take over for a few hours might just be a sanity saver.

TACKLE A BIG JOB. Our small group is giving the gift of taking on a major project together at each other's homes. Coming up soon, a single-again mom will be getting her deck powerwashed and restained. Two weeks ago, a new floor went in the family room of another small group family with the help of the other guys.

GIVE MEANINGFUL GIFTS suggest Nancy and Donald Tubesing: "Give presents (buy or make something) and give your presence (pledge your time and attention). Don't just give tickets to a cultural or sports event—plan to go along and share the experience together. Give the gift of words: affirmations, memories, thanks. Give blood. Give groceries to the food pantry. Give a mother with toddlers an afternoon of childcare. Give new books to your school library. Give a hand to a neighbor in need. Don't forget to put yourself on the gift list. Treat yourself to a gift that's just perfect for you."

Set a giving mood. Authors Tucker and Warren suggest taking a few moments before opening presents to **FOCUS ON THE SPIRIT OF CHRISTMAS**. Say a prayer as you gather around the tree. Sing carols on the porch or simply pause to be thankful for Christ's birth. They also suggest filling a box with peace and love, with an "Open me first" tag attached. Place a few sheets of tissue and a note inside the box: "This box is filled with enough peace and love to last all year! Share it generously and you will find a renewed Christmas spirit this day!"

> **Lord, You created the earth and all that is within it and gave it to humankind to enjoy. When there was nothing more for You to give, You gave Yourself. Help me to give to others as You have given so freely to me. Amen.**

All Wrapped Up

The manner of giving is worth more than the gift.

—PIERRE CORNEILLE (1606–1684), FRENCH PLAYWRIGHT

I f you don't think presentation matters, think again. "Psychologists, writers and seminar leaders all caution that we have only seven to seventeen seconds of interacting with strangers before they form an opinion of you," says David Saxby, president of Measure-X, a company that specializes in customer service and sales. "Worse yet, it takes them three times as long to change their minds about you." Image may not be everything—but it is important. Showing up for a new job interview wearing a wrinkled, unwashed pair of pants with an unmatched blouse is something you would never do. Yet, many of us have given or received a gift that wasn't dressed for presentation. You wouldn't want to disappoint the recipient before they even see the gift, would you?

When I think about all the gifts God has given us, there is no doubt that they have been painstakingly wrapped: the sky, the plants, the animals, the mountains and the seas are all breathtakingly beautiful in every detail. When it comes to giving a gift, the manner in which we present it can add or detract from the gift—no matter how great it is. Someone once told me that if we aren't up to the challenge, at least let's look like we are. That challenge works for gifts as well. The simplest and least expensive gift can leave the greatest impression if it is presented in a way that shows thoughtfulness and effort.

Some may ask, "Why wrap at all?" As authors Kristin Tucker and Rebecca Lowe Warren say, "Aside from the obvious, under wraps, our gifts become secret treasures. Colorful papers and ribbons do more than decorate. They bundle items together, protect our breakables, and tease the recipient by hiding the identity of those mysterious packages." Cynthia Yates says, "A gift from your heart will be appreciated, but so much more if you take the time to present it with care and thought."

UNWRAPPING GIFTS IS A WORLD OF FUN

Perhaps no country has been as wrapped up in gift-giving as much as Germany, a country known for its wonderful legends. In Germany Christmas gifts were called *Christ-bundles*. Seventeenth-century writings describe the contents of these bundles as including candy, sugarplums, cakes, apples and nuts. Dolls and other toys were common in addition to food. Useful items: clothes, caps, mittens, stockings and shoes also found their way into the Christ-bundles. And always tucked among the packages were objects related to teaching: ABC tables, paper, pencils and books. Lastly, attached to the bundle was the Christ-rod, which served as a pointed reminder for good behavior!

Another unique approach to presenting gifts in Germany was the custom of the Christmas Ship, in which bundles for the children were hidden. This method was also used in England to some extent but never gained popularity there. This poem by an unknown author tells of the Christmas Ship and the most important gift of Christmas:

> There gently sails a precious boat,
> It comes with rich and sacred load;
> It bears the Son of God benign,
> The loving Father's Word Divine.

Gift-giving in Russia and Poland was based on a legendary old woman called Babushka (grandmother), who gained entrance to the homes through the front door. She left beautiful enameled boxes and other wares that became family heirlooms and were passed down through the generations.

One of my assistant Patty's favorite memories of gift-giving at Christmas is the way her grandparents wrapped gifts for her mother and her mom's two sisters. The three of them loved to guess what was in a package before they opened it and were often correct in their guesses because Patty's family always exchanged lists and pretty much only gave gifts from the lists. Patty's grandparents felt that this took the fun out of opening the gifts.

Thus began the tradition of each of the daughters receiving one special "creatively" wrapped gift from their parents each year. Cousins, grandchildren and husbands looked on as Patty's mother and her sisters opened gigantic, beautifully wrapped boxes, only to find another beautifully wrapped package inside of that and so on, until finally they reached the gift. One year, Patty's grandparents actually encased the gifts in plaster-of-paris and provided a small pick axe for each of their daughters to chip away until they got to the present! No one even remembers what the presents were anymore, but they all love reminiscing about how much fun it was to watch the elaborate process of unwrapping the gifts.

How much time it must have taken her grandparents to come up with unique ways to disguise the gifts each year—but, oh, how worthwhile. Their efforts added so much anticipation and excitement to the holiday celebration as well as many cherished memories for the entire family.

SIMPLICITY MADE SIMPLE

CREATE YOUR OWN UNIQUE WRAPPING PAPER. It's as simple as grade-school art. There are so many wonderful patterns and designs of rubber stamps to use. Choose vivid paint colors and apply to plain white craft paper or butcher's paper for a crisp and clean look. Keep it simple with only one or two colors, or if you feel confident, mix it up! I also like reverse printing. Dip your pattern stamp into a dish of bleach. Then print on colored tissue or other colored paper. The bleach will remove color where you stamp, creating a unique effect. Brown package wrapping paper also works well for creating your own style.

MORE PAPER IDEAS include: newsprint paired with red ribbon, or attractive magazine pages, which are great for small items, as well as maps, pictures or pages from decorative calendars. One of my favorite wrappings is leftover wallpaper. As an interior designer I have an endless supply. But you can find remnants at your local paint and wallpaper store. It's sturdy and different from standard wrapping paper, even though you use it the same way. In particular, I love to wrap boxes in it. I purchase inexpensive lidded boxes and then dress them up with coordinating wallpapers. The paper makes the boxes sturdier. Then to the top of the lid, I add ribbons, flowers, tassels, bells, greenery—any sort of decorative detail that I happen to have. Many people have actually thought the gift was the box itself, and I had to encourage them to look inside for the real gift!

USE UNUSUAL CONTAINERS. I read about one woman who used the roll from leftover wrapping paper as a gift container for her teenage daughter's socks! She pinned together several pairs of socks and stuffed them in the roll. Imagine the fun her daughter had as she pulled and pulled one pair after the other from the tube. Containers are a great way to keep people guessing as to what the gift is. I love to fake out my husband Dave. Besides disguising gifts in containers, I write him a little clue on the tag and make him try to guess what's inside before opening. I also love using a container as the wrapping. For example, a pillowcase is perfect for so many kinds of gifts. Be sure to include the matching pillowcase as well, as an extra gift. Kitchen towels are fun and festive and make great wraps and bag stuffers.

BOX IT UP! I love hatboxes because not only are they beautiful and hold a lot of gifts but they also are great organizers for the receiver to use later. I am always on the lookout for pretty boxes. I find them at craft stores, box stores, even at some of the deep discount stores like Under a Dollar.

SOFTEN IT UP AND BUTTON UP! Fabric is another beautiful way to wrap up things. You can upholster it to a box simply by padding the box with quilt batting first. I use a spray adhesive to keep the batting in place and then wrap the fabric around and glue the edges to the inside of the box. If you sew, then you probably have an abundance of fabric pieces to choose from. If not, your local fabric store always has bins and bins of inexpensive remnants available. A scarf or bandanna is another great way to wrap a gift in a gift. I also collect buttons—who doesn't—and every time I purchase a piece of clothing I get an extra button. Anyway, they are so much fun to use as a decorative item on packages. Anchor your bows with buttons, spell out the word JOY with buttons—however you use them, they are simply fun!

BAG IT! Bags have really gained in popularity and as a result the prices just keep going up. Why not buy inexpensive, unadorned bags and decorate them yourself? Or look for bargains throughout the year. Recently, a friend told me she purchased a fifty-nine-piece all-occasion gift bag collection with matching tissue paper for $26.13. That averaged out to about fifty-seven cents a bag!

Lord, the greatest gifts may be simply wrapped,
as You were wrapped in swaddling clothes.
And the simplest of gifts may be wrapped extravagantly,
as the free gift of salvation is wrapped in the sacrifice
of Your life. I pray that all who receive my gifts will see
them as Christ-bundles of Your love. Amen.

Children and Gift-Giving

"Give good gifts to your children. . . ."

—MATTHEW 7:11 (NAS)

G od's gifts of forgiveness, love and new life come to us regardless of who we are and what we have done. If we believe that our gifts represent what God has given us, then we must, above all, hope to teach our children the profound difference between *need* and *desire*. There can be no preconditions to our giving, nor can gifts be offered as a reward or a bribe. So where does that leave Santa? Does it mean that we must destroy children's fantasies about the cheery red-suited man? Of course not.

The authors of *Celebrate the Wonder*, Tucker and Warren, say, "Santa can be a child's key to seeing the giving side of gift exchanges. As our example of a giver, he demonstrates the 'love and generosity and devotion' that parents try to instill in their children."

CHILDREN LOVE THE JOY OF GIVING

Children are smarter than we often give them credit for. They can discern a great deal about the practicalities of gift-giving while still believing in Santa. The key is in how we approach the inclusion of Santa Claus in our holiday traditions. If their image of Santa is focused on the wonder of being remembered, the mysteries of his work and the surprises he brings, they will understand that Santa doesn't bring everything they want—nor should he. Indeed, if we teach our children to be Santa's helpers and aid him in making Christmas special for those less fortunate, they will learn the art of giving as well.

Many years ago, when my goddaughter was about six, her parents divorced. It was Alexa's first Christmas with just her mother, and she was becoming a bit skeptical about the whole Santa thing. She wanted desperately to get her mother a pair of pretty earrings for Christmas but didn't have the resources. I suggested she pray and ask God to let Santa know her desire. Though a bit doubtful, she prayed. On Christmas afternoon as we were exchanging gifts at my house, Alexa found a package under the tree with a tag that said, "To: Mom, From: Santa and Alexa." Alexa's eyes were wide with amazement as her mother opened the gift—a beautiful pair of dangling earrings! Wonder, mystery and blessing were all wrapped up in that pair of earrings. Alexa's faith in God and Santa were sealed for at least another year.

"Satisfying every want and desire of a child is unhealthy, but a very hoped-for gift that will cause a stir in a child's heart and smile on *your* face is a good thing," says Cynthia Yates, author of *The Complete Guide to Creative Gift-Giving*. I agree. I still own the pair of roller skates that I desperately wanted when I was in fourth grade. For years I rented skates every Saturday morning at the rink. Receiving a brand new pair of white and silver skates for

Christmas that year was a dream come true. The good news is that they still fit me. The bad news is that everyone now uses in-line skates instead, which I am completely inept at. But just thinking about those roller skates makes me feel loved.

Guideposts writer Marjorie Holmes spoke about her family's reminiscing and the feelings of love they experienced:

> This past year, when scattered children and grandchildren came home, my oldest son produced a special treat: our old movies of Christmases past, all of which he'd transferred to videotape.
>
> Mark turned on the set, and laughing and pointing, we sat reliving the merry commotion: hanging up stockings; trimming the tree; rescuing the cat from its tangle of tinsel; church pageants and plays; little angels singing; bathrobed shepherds waving as they marched onstage; Mickie dancing in *The Nutcracker Suite*.
>
> Then, when the show was over, they all began to discuss other Christmases. "Remember the years we adopted some poor family? How everybody got busy making or buying presents? You and Daddy let us pick out the turkey, and we were so proud, but one time Mallory dropped it in the mud. Sure wish we had a shot of that!"
>
> "Me too," his sister spoke up. "But what I remember most are those Raggedy Anns and Andys we made. I helped Mother sew them, you younger kids did the stuffing and she took you along to deliver them. Boy, were you excited!"

"I was selfish," Melanie confessed. "I wanted to keep my Andy. But I was never so thrilled as when I handed him over!"

On and on they went, recalling things I'd almost forgotten. And listening, I suddenly noticed: Not once did they mention anything they got. Not even a first bicycle or special doll. Instead, to my surprise, the memories they treasured most were the fun they had in giving.

"Oh, Mother," Melanie was laughing, "doing things like that was the best part of Christmas."

"It sure was," the others agreed, expressing only one regret: How nice it would be now to see movies of those times, too.

Then several of them expressed it: Yes, but we didn't need them. We were doing something more important. The pictures were already engraved on our hearts. . . .

It doesn't get any better than that—children who have the gift of giving etched on their hearts. We all pray that our children will never know need, but we certainly want them to be aware of it. The seductions of status may entice, but soon diminishes. It is only God's abiding love in our hearts that breeds the greatest extravagance of all—charity.

SIMPLICITY MADE SIMPLE

HELP YOUR CHILDREN MAKE A LIST of people to give to this Christmas. Besides including close family and friends, neighbors and teachers, be sure to list a charity or needy family as well. Together, take the time to talk about each person on the list and remember times you shared with them. This helps make the people more relevant to their lives and will also help inspire gift ideas for each.

HELP YOUR CHILDREN "PLAY SANTA" by giving gifts in secret. This is a perfect way to teach the gift of giving by placing the focus on the giving and not on the giver. Family members and friends will enjoy such a gift. But it's also a great way to give to a neighbor or needy family without making them feel obliged in any way or uncomfortable.

GUIDE YOUR CHILDREN'S GIFT CHOICES. Explain that a gift should express your care and desire to make Christmas special. Personalized greetings mean a lot and don't have to cost a lot. For example, if you're handy with a computer, creating a DVD collage of pictures or a collection of music is a great way to get a child's creative juices flowing. Both my brother and my sister have made music CDs for me. I cherish them and enjoy listening to them. Although they each chose completely different music, each collection is absolutely perfect for me! Grandparents and aunts and uncles especially appreciate artwork by the children. Since I don't have children of my own, receiving a handmade gift from a child is always a special treat for me.

GIVE THE GIFT OF LABOR. There are so many ways you can give this gift. Offer to help a neighbor clean up a yard, rake leaves, shovel snow or even decorate the house for Christmas. Caring for pets or plants during holiday travels can mean a lot. Babysitting, grocery shopping and cleaning windows are all simply perfect gifts that mean a lot.

HELP CHILDREN SHOP. Children love giving something they have picked out themselves. Many churches and schools arrange a Santa store where children can shop. If you don't have the store in your area—consider starting one. Our local Christian school organized a group of volunteers that craft, buy and plan for the children's shop all year long. Then in early December the store is open for an entire week. And it's not just for children—anyone can shop there. My friend Jan bought me the most beautiful handmade wooden Christmas partridge and pear tree. It is simple but elegant, and it fits perfectly on my kitchen windowsill every year. Another year, I received a beautiful little claypotted candle that was painted a pretty shade of blue with silver wash and a white bow, which sits on the corner of my desk. Other ideas that help to stretch a child's budget are: import stores such as Ten Thousand Villages (a missionary fund-raising project of the Mennonite Church, www.tenthousandvillages.com), magazine counters, candle stores, road maps, seeds, cookie cutters, spiced teas, measuring tapes or even a bowl of seashells.

Evaluate your own gift-giving. Nothing teaches as much as what we do. If we tell our children that gifts don't have to be expensive to be thoughtful, but then they hear us comment that we "haven't spent enough," they will learn that gifts must be expensive. Make sure your actions match your personal values. Start by shortening your own list of "I wants." Then plan to make a contribution to a charity or someone less fortunate than yourself. **PURCHASE ONLY GIFTS THAT ARE MADE OR SOLD TO HELP OTHERS** such as those bought through nonprofit organizations. Give the gift of your time to a hospital or nursing home. This can be a family or even a neighborhood affair. If you're having a party, simply ask each guest to bring something that can be placed in a gift basket for the homebound, hospital patients or even prison inmates. You could also hold a garage sale or craft bazaar to raise money for world hunger, cancer patients or your favorite charitable organization.

Lord, sometimes I feel that the needs of others
are so great that my small contribution is worthless.
But deep inside of me remains the desire to give.
Please bless what is in my hand to share with others and
help it fill the longing of someone's heart. Amen.

The Hard-to-Buy-For Crowd

Verily I say unto you, Inasmuch as ye have
done it unto one of the least of these . . .
ye have done it unto me.

—MATTHEW 25:40 (KJV)

Selecting gifts for the elderly, especially those living in a nursing home, creates a unique challenge. After all, how many bottles of perfume or cologne can one person possibly use? Gadgets, knickknacks or silly gag gifts get to be a bit tiresome. Out of frustration, most seniors simply say, "Don't buy me anything!" The reality is that they don't want any more clutter. "They don't need stuff," said gerontologist and assistant professor of psychology Lee Stadtlander. "They have stuff."[22]

The real key to selecting useful gifts is as simple as talking with the person about what she or he could use. If she is living in a nursing home, check with the staff. They often have a better idea than anyone else with regard to the real needs of residents. For many elderly, the best gift you can give is a visit or a phone call.

When Stadtlander asked a group of elderly women she was working with what they wanted during the holidays, they said that they really wanted more interaction with their families.

IT'S POSSIBLE TO FIND A "PERFECT" GIFT FOR EVERYONE

Lisa Hallaman, a geriatric specialist and director of the Montana State University Young at Heart exercise program for the elderly, agreed. She said, "The best thing anyone can do is spend time. But don't make it just a holiday visit. Make it something you commit to on a regular basis, either for those who can't get out or for those who don't have family near."

Stadtlander suggested giving the elderly person a calendar indicating which days you will come to visit throughout the year. Those days can be made special by including a lunch together or simply sitting and talking. "Even [for] patients with dementia, the best thing anyone can do is sit, hold their hand and allow them to talk," said Hallaman. Sadly, we assume that nursing home residents have a lot of human contact, but the reality is that it is not very often that anyone has or takes the time to just sit with them on an emotional level and touch them.

Both Hallaman and Stadtlander agree that offering to help the elderly send a card to a friend or family member is a great way to not only help them stay in contact, but to also help them receive lots of mail in return. Postage stamps or gift certificates for a styling salon or barbershop are also fine gift ideas. The elderly like to reminisce. So a scrapbook of their special events with pictures, articles and other mementos of fond memories is a tangible way for them to remember and share with others. Grandparents love to brag about their grandchildren. Making a scrapbook of various activities, school papers and pictures of special events like birthday parties is a wonderful way to keep grandparents in the know while also giving them an entertaining way to share their stories with others.

Sometimes, finding the perfect gift is simply about learning to stretch your imagination in a different direction as Guideposts writer Terry Helwig did one year:

> As I make my Christmas gift list, I sigh deeply. What should I give? Money? Books? Candy? Sometimes I find the *perfect* gift, like the ceramic angel holding a rabbit for my friend Linda who collects rabbits. But finding the perfect gift is more the exception than the rule.
>
> Oddly enough, when later I'm opening the mail, I come across one of the many requests from a charity. I think of my unfinished Christmas gift list . . . What if, for those people who have everything, I were to make a contribution to a charity as my gift to them? The idea excites me.
>
> For my dear friend Denise who is blessed with two children, Alyce and Christian, I could donate to a hospital (like St. Jude) or help feed a child in another part of the world. For my friend Karen who loves animals, I could donate to an organization that prevents cruelty to animals or send money to save dolphins or whales. For my friend Betsy who runs a store that sells environmentally friendly products, I could donate to an organization trying to preserve the rain forests.
>
> My daughter's school is collecting children's mittens and socks for a Native American mission. Somehow, I can't think

of a more perfect gift than if someone were to write to me and say, "Terry, my gift to you this year is a donation to a local mission. In honor of you and our friendship, five little children will be wearing warm, fuzzy mittens."

Maybe it isn't that hard to find the perfect gift after all!

SIMPLICITY MADE SIMPLE

SPECIAL GIFTS FOR OLDER PEOPLE can really be a blessing. Simply take some time to think about particular challenges they may have. Then look for some solutions. For example, if a loved one has trouble projecting her voice, then choose a small microphone that can be worn on a lightweight necklace. Specially designed bottle-, jar- and can-openers can make the task of opening a jar so much easier for someone with arthritis. Some telephones, which can be programmed for speed dialing, have large buttons that can accommodate photos of people who are frequently called—this is perfect for seniors who sometimes have memory problems. Talking clocks and talking thermometers are another great choice for someone with failing eyesight.

Large magnifiers are great for anyone over fifty! They make instructions, telephone books, watches or buttons on the VCR so much easier to see. Speaking of VCRs, many of the elderly don't even own one of these. It can be the perfect present. Add copies of a few of their favorite movies—and you have a gift that keeps on giving. In fact, many older people have outdated electronic appliances. Not only is an old toaster or coffeemaker potentially dangerous, but they may prohibit older folks from enjoying some of the newer technologies on the market. Consider changing an old thermostat to one with a large lighted digital readout and two simple up or down arrows for controlling. Also be sure to install it no more than forty-eight inches above the floor so that a person in a wheelchair can easily read and reach it. When **REPLACING OLD APPLIANCES,** such as a stove, be sure that the controls are on the *front* rather than the top or back so as to make them easier to read and reach as well.

FEED THEM. Sadly, as we age, often we lose the desire to cook from scratch. This can lead to poor eating habits and nutritional deficiencies. So why not arrange to have precooked meals delivered each week. That way all the recipient has to do to have a great wholesome meal is heat it up!

Help them walk. **FOLDING CANES THAT ILLUMINATE** in the dark are a great gift for anyone who depends on a cane to get around. Moreover, users of these canes can easily be located at nighttime, which is a very important feature for safety and convenience.

HELP THEM PLAY. For bridge players, there are decks of cards with large numbers and automatic card shufflers and cardholders. This makes it easy for everyone to play. Puzzles are an excellent way to help keep stiff fingers nimble. Just remember to choose shapes and sizes that are easy to see and handle. Word Find, Upword, Scrabble and crossword puzzles in large print are other game ideas that keep older minds sharp.

Give the gift of sight and hearing. For those struggling to see, give the gift of audio books, magazines or radio shows. Offer to be a personal secretary—write letters, pay bills, whatever. A pedicure or manicure is not only welcome for both genders, but is a necessity. My friend Donna is a manicurist and goes into nursing homes twice a week. It is a true gift of love. For the hearing impaired, a TV set with a built-in decoder for closed-caption broadcasts is a wonderful idea. A flashing or vibrating alarm clock, doorbell, smoke alarm and telephone are all **ESSENTIAL GIFTS**.

Pay attention and always assess the individual situation. Some of our elderly *are* in need. They may need money, food or a ride to the doctor but they probably would never tell you or ask you for help. **GIVE THEM THE BEST OF BOTH WORLDS**: the help they need and the gift of friendship.

Father, when I don't think I have time to add service to my schedule, then I know I am too busy. Help me to clear my life of what is unnecessary in order to serve both the old and the young who cannot serve themselves. And when I do, may they feel Your love for them. Amen.

PART FIVE

Celebrating Life

THERE ARE MANY DAYS that have been set aside throughout the year for celebration. Digging into the history of why we celebrate certain days brings more meaning to these holidays, so in this final section of the book I will share some of the insights that I found about these days that have been set apart from our routine. We have been given many opportunities to call together our family and friends to give thanks for all that God has done for us. As you read the various tips and ideas on how to celebrate the other holidays of the year, I hope you will be inspired to create your own memorials and celebrate more of life along the way.

Valentine's Day

My dear children, let's not just talk about love;

let's practice real love.

—1 JOHN 3:18 (MSG)

Valentine's Day was first observed in the Middle Ages. We celebrate it to honor St. Valentine. But it's not clear *which* St. Valentine we are celebrating. You see, there are eight different St. Valentine's. The most popular story is about the St. Valentine who was a priest during the third century in Rome under the rule of Emperor Claudius II.

It is believed that this St. Valentine is the patron saint of romance because of his role in subverting the rule of Emperor Claudius II. During this time period, Claudius had determined that single men made better soldiers than married ones. Logically, he took the step of outlawing marriage for young men as he wanted these people to focus on serving him as soldiers. Of course, many young men weren't exactly thrilled with this prospect. Hence, St. Valentine decided to engage in some civil disobedience; he continued his practice of performing marriages for young lovers. However, once Claudius found out what St. Valentine was doing, let's just say he wasn't very pleased and had St. Valentine imprisoned. While in prison awaiting his beheading, St. Valentine, according to one story, fell in love with the jailer's daughter. In his parting letter to her, he sealed the fate of the day by signing, "From Your Valentine."

In memory of this martyred saint, we honor love. It is one of the most celebrated holidays with more than 850 million commercial valentines being exchanged each year. Valentine's Day is a time to acknowledge loved ones. Valentines themselves have been around since the fifteenth century. The holiday's love letters that we exchange today have origins in nineteenth century as fancy paper designed with flowers and hearts. Back then, people wrote their own messages. In fact, in 1840 valentine cards were actually works of art. Often they were hand-painted and adorned with silk, lace and fresh flowers. Even glass ornamentation was used.

Esther Allen Howland is credited as the first person to sell and mass-produce lavish valentines. She is known as the "Mother of the American valentine." In 1847, she persuaded her father, who was a stationer, to order a supply of large blank lace-paper sheets and other decorative materials from England. She proceeded to make a small assortment of sample cards. She then persuaded her brother, who worked as a traveling salesman for their father, to take her card with him.

When he returned with five thousand orders, she set up shop in a spare room of the family's home, grabbed a few of her friends to help her, and began the first assembly-line production of American commercial valentines. What is truly astounding is that over one hundred and fifty years ago she was selling them for five and ten dollars a card! Despite this incredibly high price, her cards were extremely popular—popular enough to earn her one hundred thousand dollars a year. Simply gazing at an old Victorian valentine card is to return to a more romantic era.

Sarah Ban Breathnach, author of *Mrs. Sharp's Traditions—Reviving Victorian Family Celebrations of Comfort and Joy* and the best-selling *Simple Abundance*, says, "Perhaps no memento so perfectly captures the essence of an entire epoch as the valentine does for the Victorians. Hidden within the undulating paper curves of these charmingly conceived, lovingly crafted tokens of affection—the more elaborate the better—lie fascinating clues to the gilded age in which the valentine was transformed from mere ephemera into art."[23]

EXPAND YOUR CIRCLE OF LOVE

I am just amazed at how this holiday has transitioned from the martyrdom of a sweet saint to an outpouring of cards, gifts, flowers and chocolate. Perhaps it's simply because we are all in love with love. And that just might be the right place to begin. Shouldn't our expressions of love reflect our values?

Deep down in your heart, what is most important about those you love? What do you cherish above all? Is it their devotion to God and living lives of integrity and compassion? If so, be sure to express it. Is it the little things they remember to do? Be sure to let them know how much you appreciate that. Ultimately, it is the expression of our love in simple yet meaningful ways that make our loved ones feel good—very good. Guideposts writer Pam Kidd wrote the following story about new and interesting ways to lift people's spirits on Valentine's Day:

> For most of us, Valentine's Day is a time when we exchange
> loving sentiments with those closest to us. Already, I know that

before the day ends, my husband David will surprise me with some sweet gift and a card that expresses his love. And, of course, I have a card and a special surprise with his name attached. Our family valentine exchange extends to our children Brock and Keri, to our mothers and to others we hold especially dear.

But recently, I learned that once the traditions were quite different than they are today. In earlier times, valentines, love notes and other tokens of affection were always sent anonymously.

That sparks an idea: Why shouldn't I be someone's secret admirer today? I could send flowers to that once-in-a-lifetime grammar school teacher who practically doubled my confidence level the year I was in her class. Attaching a simple thank-you note signed "one of your grateful students" would most likely speak for a hundred others besides me.

I know a little girl who loves Barbie dolls. Just suppose I made a tiny valentine and dropped it off in her mailbox. "To Barbie . . . From a Secret Admirer." Wouldn't that bring a sparkle to her eye?

And that lonely man I know who lost his wife. I wonder . . . if I took the time to bake a pie today, and left it on his doorstep with an unsigned note, wouldn't that make him feel less lonely?

Wonderful "valentine opportunities" are all around, it seems. With the smallest effort, it becomes a day for widening my circle of love.

Now that's what I call active love!

SIMPLICITY MADE SIMPLE

GIVE THE BEST FOR LESS. Nancy Twigg, author of *Celebrate Simply*, says, "Simplifying does not mean you scrimp on the generous outpouring of your love." There's nothing wrong with candy, flowers and dining out, but by putting your creativity to work, you can bypass traditional gifts and give a unique and eloquent expression of your love for less money (and more heart). Twigg suggests giving an "I Love You Because . . ." jar. Fill it with individual slips of paper, each listing something you love and appreciate about your sweetheart. Or consider giving your honey a break from housework or yard work. You could also volunteer to help them tackle a mountain of a project that he or she has been putting off. The point is simply to make your loved one feel extraordinary.

Make your own valentines. **HOMEMADE VALENTINES** are so much more interesting and more heartfelt too. Why not pick a day and make it a family affair. Elizabeth Berg, author of *Family Traditions: Celebrations for Holidays and Everyday*, says, "Often, siblings who don't ordinarily get along very well will work harmoniously on a crafts project. While you're cutting and pasting, share stories of romance: how you met your first boyfriend/girlfriend; what you love about your current flame. Older children, especially, will enjoy this." The valentines you make can be as simple or elaborate as you like. Just be sure that every member of the family gets to participate. The goal is not perfection but enjoyment of each other's company. You may even want to include your children's friends—and make it more fun for everyone.

CREATE MESSAGE VALENTINES. This can be done simply by using words and/or pictures cut from magazines to put a message on a blank sheet of paper or cut-out heart. For children who don't yet read, use valentine stickers.

Object valentines are another fun craft that will express your love in an unusual way. Let everyday objects glued or taped on a heart help convey your message. For example, Barg writes, a piece of wrapped candy can say, "I'm sweet on you." Pine needles let someone know, "I pine for you." And a penny can say, "I'm not worth one cent without you."

Give the gesture of love. Let Valentine's Day be the day you **SHOW LOVE TO OTHERS**. Visit a nursing home with valentines and lots of goodies. Most importantly, simply take the time to sit and talk with the residents. Or do as Pam Kidd suggested and bake a pie for the elderly guy down the street. Donate food to a shelter. Simply reach out and give a little TLC—tender loving care.

WRITE A LOVE LETTER. Talk about the first time you met. Let him know all the things that you like about him, both then and now. If you are writing to children, tell them about the day they were born or something endearing they did. Elizabeth Berg suggests getting sloppy and sentimental. Write like a Victorian. Or simply and honestly express your love. The truth of your declaration is what matters most.

Lord, forgive me for looking out for my own needs
more than I do for others. Cleanse me of the desire
to be loved rather than to love. Cause Your love
for others to grow in me, and help me keep the spirit
of Valentine's Day alive all year. Amen.

Easter

"Do not be afraid. . . . he has risen. . . ."

—MATTHEW 28:5–6 (RSV)

E aster was the first high holiday of the Christian faith, and it came into exis-
tence very early in the history of Christianity. I believe it is the greatest day
on the church calendar because it celebrates the biggest miracle ever—Christ's
death and Resurrection.

Easter is not just a one-day event but it includes a season called Lent that
lasts forty days. Forty is a fairly significant number in the Bible: Moses spent
forty days on Mt. Sinai, the Israelites wandered in the desert for forty years, and
Christ spent forty days in the wilderness as well as forty hours in the tomb. Lent
is intended to be a time of meditating on the meaning of life. It should be a time
to bring our lives into closer communion with God and also to bring us closer to
those we love. Rachel Hartman, author of *The Joys of Easter*, put it this way: "As
we learn from the Master who washed His disciples' feet, may we put into practice 'by love serve one another' (Galatians 5:13) in our homes."

Ash Wednesday marks the beginning of Lent. Ashes that are made from branches of brushwood or palms from Palm Sunday, the previous year, are placed as a mark on the foreheads of the faithful. They are meant to be a reminder: Thou art dust and unto dust thou shalt return. Palm Sunday commemorates the triumphant return of Christ to Jerusalem, where jubilant crowds greeted him waving palm fronds. It is also the beginning of the final week of Lent. Each day of Holy Week recalls a day in the Passion of Christ.

A SEASON OF NEW LIFE

For many years I was part of a Christian drama team. During the Easter season we would present a full-length musical drama about the Passion of Christ. Most years I was the director. But for two years they asked me to play the role of Mary, Christ's mother. I wish I could convey to you how powerfully that role affected me. Our portrayal of events was very real. The crucifixion and the nailing of Christ to the cross was heart wrenching. I found myself reeling in pain. Overwhelmed, I could only imagine how the real Mary must have felt. That experience forever changed the way I see Easter.

All the days of that incredible week led up to the most exceptional day of all—the Resurrection of our Lord. Christ's victory over death and the new life we receive in Him is joyously triumphant. The joy of His Resurrection has echoed through the centuries. Easter is a time of glory. Author Nancy Twigg says, "When celebrated against the backdrop of the darkness and mourning of Holy Week, Easter becomes a glorious proclamation of hope and God's love. That is why it is so important to understand the significance of the entire Easter season." You cannot fully experience the exuberance of the Resurrection if you have not tasted the sorrows.

I like to think of Easter as the culmination of the joy that began at

Christmas. But Easter is also a beginning—a beginning of new life. Rachel Hartman says, "Fear and discouragement are much a part of the human condition, but Easter took the sting out of death, replaced discouragement with hope and fear with love." Christ upset everything that first Easter morning. He willingly accepted being condemned to die a horrible death for a crime he didn't commit, without complaint. In fact, he even asked God to forgive those who condemned Him—unheard of! Then, after being killed in plain view of hundreds of witnesses, He arose from the dead—again, unheard of! His death and resurrection changed our world forever.

Truly the real message of Easter is, "Fear not." Guideposts writer Keith Miller discovered both the joy and the courage of Easter and has learned to apply it to his life:

> For many years I used to think about God and wonder if He were real, and if so, what He was like. As a child, I'd heard He was like Jesus, but the Sunday schools I was exposed to seemed to picture Jesus as a sissy no one would want to be with, or a father, which meant that He traveled a lot and didn't have much time for me, or as a giant policeman in plain clothes who was "on my case."
>
> Over the years my picture of Jesus changed. But it wasn't until I read the Gospel of Matthew and put myself in Matthew's place that I really found Him. Here is what I imagine Matthew must have experienced on Easter Sunday. . . .
>
> I have seen Jesus alive! Suddenly, He appeared right in the midst of us. I've never been so confused. But I touched Him. So I have to believe.

Yet what did His dying on the cross mean? What was this stuff about being raised from the dead? When and where was God's kingdom coming? And then it hit me. We'd misunderstood! We were not to look for a political king who would take over the government. Jesus was trying to tell us that God's rule was going to be a personal kingdom within ourselves, which would reach clear across the world! What Jesus had done when He walked into my experience, and John's and Peter's, was to put down a bridge from God to us, a bridge into the inner loneliness and fear in which I lived. "Listen," He had told us, "God loves you and you're never going to be alone again! He's with you and I'm with you."

Now, as His follower, I am to put my life down as a plank across the separation into other people's lives, so that God can somehow walk across my vulnerability into their fear and loneliness. God can lead them out of their caves of hiding and put their hands in the hands of other lonely little children. They, and we, will form a new and intimate community, the family of God, the church of Jesus Christ.

SIMPLICITY MADE SIMPLE

CELEBRATE THE RESURRECTION. Nancy Twigg suggests accomplishing this by doing the kinds of things Jesus came to earth to do. "Extend God's love to others by visiting the elderly and sick, gathering up clothing to take to a homeless shelter, or making and delivering food baskets to families in need."

Turn the Easter celebration into **A LEARNING EXPERIENCE**. I love learning about other cultures and their traditions. Perhaps it's because I come from such a multicultural family. In Poland, Easter is celebrated passionately. Thousands of people gather on Easter Saturday carrying their Easter baskets of eggs and other foods to the churches to be blessed. Eggs are a natural symbol of birth, new life, resurrection and renewal. They have been used all over the world as a traditional Easter symbol. Many Europeans create beautiful, intricate traditional Easter patterns on eggs. The oldest surviving decorated egg was found in a Roman sarcophagus in the city of Worms (now part of Germany). It dates back to the fourth century A.D. The wearing of brand-new clothes is said to represent a personal rebirth. New suits and Easter bonnets, adorned with flowers of spring, represent the new person we can each become. In Europe the congregation used to take an Easter walk through the fields or an open place, all dressed in their new clothes. Hence—the Easter Parade. Sometimes a candle or crucifix led the procession as they sang hymns. The Easter bunny is believed to have originated in the sixteenth century in German literature. When Germans immigrated to America, they brought this tradition of *Osterhase* (Easter bunny) with them. Children would make nests in their hats and bonnets and the folkloric rabbit would place colored eggs in them. Eventually the homemade nests developed into baskets.

ROLL EGGS WITH YOUR CHILDREN—it's a time-honored White House tradition. Dolly Madison is usually credited with this tradition, which started around 1809. Originally, families with young children would roll Easter eggs, colored by children of the president and his staff, across the lawn of the Capitol. In 1876 President Rutherford B. Hayes attempted to stop this event because of the toll it took on the grounds. But he was confronted by children armed with Easter baskets in protest of the cancellation. The president and his wife were charmed by the children and reinstated the tradition in 1878. Ever since, children along with their parents roll eggs on the south lawn of the White House. As a souvenir each child receives a wooden egg signed by the president and first lady.

MAKE AN EASTER WREATH. The joy and hope of the Easter Resurrection has been symbolized for centuries by lambs, lilies and crosses. Why not incorporate some of these symbols into a decorative wreath for your holiday display? Start with a grape ivy wreath (it can be purchased at a craft store) to represent the crown of thorns, which Christ wore. Then decorate it with angels, lilies and gold ribbon. The angels announced Christ's resurrection. The lilies symbolize new life. And gold symbolizes triumph.

Decorate for the season. Use colors as a significant reminder of Christ's love and sacrifice. Purple is a sign of wealth, power and royalty. It has come to represent our Lord and King. It is also used as a color of repentance. Consider using it in your table linens. Combine it with white, the symbol of Christ's purity. Red is used to commemorate the death of a martyr. It is also the color of fire—a symbol of the Holy Spirit. Use red candles throughout your home as a symbol of both Christ's death and the coming of the Holy Spirit. Palms make a lovely addition to your holiday table. Decorate the backs of your dining chairs with palm branches and lilies. Start with the palms as a base. Then add lilies and gold branches or other trim. Simply tie them to the chair with white and gold ribbon for **A SYMBOLICALLY BEAUTIFUL EASTER DECORATION**.

Lord, You laid down Your life for ours—and now
You live with us and in us—promising our eternal life.
I praise You and give You thanks for all that
the Easter season teaches us. Amen.

Mother's Day and Father's Day

"Honor your father and your mother. . . ."

—EXODUS 20:12 (NIV)

Mother's Day has an interesting origin. In England, the fourth Sunday of Lent is known as Mothering Sunday, a custom that arose during the Middle Ages, based on the verse that says, "But Jerusalem which is above is free, which is the mother of us all [Galatians 4:26, KJV]." This day was set aside to "go a-mothering," which was a day meant for young people who had to live away from home—in apprenticeship or domestic service—to return home to visit their mother church and their biological mothers. It occurred in the middle of Lent on a day called Laetare Sunday (from the Latin verb *laetare*, meaning "to be joyful"). They brought presents to their mothers as well as to the church.

Mother's Day as we now know it dates back to 1907 in Philadelphia, Pennsylvania, when Miss Anna Jarvis, one of eleven children, held a service to honor her mother. On the anniversary of her mother's death, she arranged for a church service to honor all mothers. By 1914, the idea was so popular that

President Woodrow Wilson declared the second Sunday in May to be Mother's Day. Americans were asked to display the flag as a public expression of their love and reverence for the mothers of our country.

It is said that Father's Day formally preceded Mother's Day by four years. Mrs. John Bruce Dodd of Spokane, Washington, suggested to the Spokane Ministerial Association that they approve the third Sunday in June be set aside for honoring fathers. She and her siblings had been raised by their father after the death of their mother. It was first celebrated on her father's birthday, June 19, in 1910. However, you might be surprised to know that it wasn't official until 1966, when President Lyndon Johnson proclaimed the third Sunday in June as Father's Day. And it didn't become a permanent national observance until 1972, when President Richard Nixon made it so.

Did you know that the rose is the official flower for Father's Day? Red roses are a tribute to a living father, white ones for remembrance. The tradition of pink and white carnations as Mother's Day flowers is something I remember from my childhood. I was around eleven years old when I discovered that a pink carnation was to be worn for a living mother and a white one if your mother was dead. I spent the entire day in dread of meeting someone with a white carnation. This tradition was established in memory of President William McKinley who always wore a white carnation, his mother's favorite.

HONOR IS PRAISE DESERVED

Honoring our mother and father is expected. But for some it can be hard, especially if our parents haven't been the best of role models. *In Family Traditions* Elizabeth Berg addresses this issue beautifully: "Not all of us, of course, had idyllic relationships with our parents. There may have been very painful parts of our past with them that we have had to learn to forgive (or are still trying to). But as we are not perfect, neither are our parents—after all, they came from parents with their own problems. One of the tasks of adulthood is coming to terms with the pain we endured in childhood, whether it was a little or a lot. To that end, we work toward loving our parents as best we can, regardless of circumstances. It is never too late for that, and it is always worth doing." I agree. I had some very serious issues with my own father. I can tell you from personal experience that there is nothing more freeing than to forgive.

Honoring our parents on these special days is wonderful—but it is even more important to remember our parents throughout the year. The older I get, the more grateful I am for my mother. I love her and tell her every time I speak with her. It's so easy to do and it means so much. I enjoy how Guideposts writer Jeff Japinga expresses his appreciation for his dad:

> They say Father's Day is set aside to honor dads, and that makes sense. I'm not a dad yet, just a son, but still I know all about what it means to be a dad. You see, my dad taught me.
>
> He taught me in our backyard on 26th Street in Holland, Michigan, where the clothesline pole was third base and the sandbox first. He taught me the night I heard him say into the telephone, "I can't go, my son is sick." He taught me the night it snowed so hard I didn't get home from my date until 1:30 A.M. and found him still up waiting. (After chewing me out, he told me how concerned he had been.) He taught me about jump shots and a sense of humor and how to live as if God made a difference in your life.
>
> So what does a kid like me who can shoot a jump shot but

has never had to deal with children's headaches know about being a father? Just what my dad taught: that being a father means having one day in your honor, but giving your child three hundred sixty-five Son's Days.

Yep, every day, I got a present from my dad: *himself.* And that's why, when I get to be a father myself, I know I'm going to be ready.

SIMPLICITY MADE SIMPLE

MAKE YOUR PARENT'S DAY SPECIAL BY MAKING A DATE! Simply find something for the two of you to do such as a play, movie, ball game or a special restaurant for lunch or dinner. Make your mom or dad feel young again by taking her or him to someplace she/he loved as a child—perhaps the zoo or the playground in the old neighborhood. Just be sure to leave plenty of time for talking.

GET THEIR HOUSE IN ORDER. Hiring a handyman for a day to do all the little things that are in need of repair is a great gift. Have leaky faucets fixed, repair broken windows, replace weather stripping, paint a room or simply have someone trim shrubbery. I recently hired someone to wash down my mother's ceilings and walls as well as the kitchen cabinets and hanging light fixtures. She was thrilled and is thoroughly enjoying her clean house.

Do something personal. Enlarge a favorite photo or transfer old movies onto VCR tape or DVDs. **MAKE A MEMORY COLLAGE** with old photos, objects, ticket stubs and letters—whatever you can find that is a good-remembrance symbol. Have new luxury towels monogrammed. Repair and/or clean an old piece of jewelry. I have done this twice for my mom and she was very appreciative.

GIVE YOUR PARENTS A MINIVACATION. Arrange for an overnight getaway to visit friends or relatives in another city. You can join them or simply make the reservations. If there is someplace or someone they would like to visit within a few hours' drive, hire a car service to take them there. This is especially good if your parent doesn't like to fly.

FEED THEM. I read about one woman who gave her dad the gift of his choice of homemade pastries for a year. Each month she would ask him what he wanted as his treat and she made it. He felt honored every time because he knew she was taking time out of her busy schedule to do something just for him. You might also arrange to make a home-cooked meal once a week. If you live too far away to do this yourself, make arrangements with a local restaurant or catering service.

Give them **GIFT CERTIFICATES**. I usually find this too impersonal but my mother loves getting a gift certificate to her favorite clothing store. She simply wouldn't take money from her own budget for such a luxury, but she delights in being able to shop without worry. Other ideas are long-distance phone cards, a cell phone with unlimited long-distance calling, cable service, or even a magazine subscription that focuses on a particular hobby or passion.

Lord, thank You for my parents. You scripted valuable lessons into their life stories that when learned can make my path easier. Bless the memories that I have of them and direct me on a good path through illustrations of their lives. Help me to honor them in the decisions that I now make. Amen.

Thanksgiving

Let us come before him with thanksgiving. . . .

—PSALM 95:2 (NIV)

As I began to think about Thanksgiving I couldn't help but wonder how we came to celebrate it as a national holiday. Yes, we all know the story about the pilgrims and the Wampanoag Indians, but how did we come to make this reenactment into a national holiday? There is quite a progression in its history, but one thing that certainly stands out is that Abraham Lincoln declared it a national holiday on October 3, 1863. Have you ever read his proclamation? I hadn't. And it intrigued me to know that this proclamation happened in the midst of the Civil War.

We were at war, yet Lincoln was declaring a holiday of Thanksgiving? It seemed incongruous to me. So I searched and found Lincoln's proclamation and I personally think that everyone who celebrates Thanksgiving should consider reading it at the dinner table this year. I hope it gives you a new perspective and a renewed appreciation for all that God has indeed blessed us with.

Taken from the collection of Lincoln's papers in the Library of America series:

The year that is drawing towards its close has been filled with the blessings of fruitful fields and healthful skies. To these bounties, which are so constantly enjoyed that we are prone to forget the source from which they come, others have been added, which are of so extraordinary a nature, that they cannot fail to penetrate and soften even the heart which is habitually insensible to the ever watchful providence of Almighty God. In the midst of a civil war of unequalled magnitude and severity, which has sometimes seemed to foreign States to invite and to provoke their aggression, peace has been preserved with all nations, order has been maintained, the laws have been respected and obeyed, and harmony has prevailed everywhere except in the theatre of military conflict; while that theatre has been greatly contracted by the advancing armies and navies of the Union. Needful diversions of wealth and of strength from the fields of peaceful industry to the national defence, have not arrested the plough, the shuttle, or the ship; the axe had enlarged the borders of our settlements, and the mines, as well of iron and coal as of the precious metals, have yielded even more abundantly than heretofore. Population has steadily increased, notwithstanding the waste that has been made in the camp, the siege and the battlefield; and the country, rejoicing in the consciousness of augmented strength and vigor, is permitted to expect continuance of years with a large increase of freedom.

No human counsel hath devised nor hath any mortal hand worked out these great things. They are the gracious gifts of the Most High God, who, while dealing with us in anger for our sins, hath nevertheless remembered mercy. It has seemed to me fit and proper that they should be solemnly, reverently and gratefully acknowledged as with one heart and voice by the whole American People. I do therefore invite my fellow citizens in every part of the United States, and also those who are at sea and those who are sojourning in foreign lands, to set apart and observe the last Thursday of November next, as a day of Thanksgiving and Praise to our beneficent Father who dwelleth in the Heavens. And I recommend to them that while offering up the ascriptions justly due to Him for such singular deliverances and blessings, they do also, with humble penitence for our national perverseness and disobedience, commend to His tender care all those who have become widows, orphans, mourners or sufferers in the lamentable civil strife in which we are unavoidably engaged, and fervently implore the interposition of the Almighty Hand to heal the wounds of the nation and to restore it as soon as may be consistent with the Divine purposes to the full enjoyment of peace, harmony, tranquillity and Union.

SOMETHING MORE THAN TURKEY AND PIE

Nancy Twigg, in *Celebrate Simply*, says that "although each of us has a multitude of reasons to be thankful, we often tend to celebrate Thanksgiving more out of habit than heartfelt gratitude." I hope that after reading Lincoln's proclamation that you will be aware of the ever-watchful providence of God in your life. I hope that we will learn to be grateful every day for His abundance, not just once a year. Our annual celebration should be a culmination of all our days of praise and deep appreciation for the blessings God has bestowed on us.

Brock Kidd wrote about how he discovered, while away at college, that Thanksgiving Day is not just about turkey and pumpkin pie:

> I used to think Thanksgiving was about pilgrims and pumpkin pie. My freshman year in college changed my mind.
>
> By mid-November, students were decorating all over campus, and the cafeteria menu offered pumpkin pie. An important final paper was due, and I decided to forego the holiday in favor of research. *I'll just celebrate it up here*, I thought. The right ingredients for Thanksgiving were all around me. Yet I was miserably homesick, and in my head I kept hearing:
>
> > *Over the river and through the woods,*
> > *To Grandmother's house we go . . .*
>
> At the last minute, unable to bear the self-imposed exile, I caught a late-night bus home. . . .
>
> *Finally, I'm home.* My head is bowed for my father's Thanksgiving prayer. "God, thank You for a full table and a family to share it with . . ." he begins. I squint one eye half-open and peep around. Uncles, aunts, cousins. *Joy.*
>
> I breathe deeply, savoring the aroma of my grandmother's

cornbread dressing browning in the oven. The massive turkey waits on the table. Caramel, apple and pumpkin pie, prune cake, banana pudding are on the sideboard. All the ingredients, just as I had imagined. But the food doesn't seem so important now.

After the prayer, my grandmother squeezes my hand. "Brockwell, we've missed you. We wouldn't be a family without you."

I feel myself growing up a bit as I stand there with my grandmother's arm around me. From now on, Thanksgiving will be a lot less about a table full of turkey and trimmings, and a lot more about giving thanks for the people around the table.

Perhaps, as we all do a little growing up, our appreciation for God and country will increase. Have a blessed Thanksgiving.

S I M P L I C I T Y   M A D E   S I M P L E

Follow the example set by the pilgrims and President Lincoln. **LET THE SPIRIT OF GRATITUDE BE THE MOTIVATION** behind your festivities. Nancy Twigg reminds us that "the pilgrims celebrated a true spirit of gratitude. Only about half of the original Mayflower travelers actually survived the first winter in the New World." And if it had not been for the help of the Wampanoag Indians, many others may have died as well. The bountiful harvest celebration was the best way the pilgrims knew to honor their good fortune and thank the Indians as well.

Make Thanksgiving more meaningful. Thanksgiving began as a holy day, created by a community of God-fearing puritans sincere in their desire to set aside one day each year especially to thank the Lord for His many blessings. One of the simplest ways to revive this attitude is to have family members write down one thing they are thankful for from the past year. You can have them write it on a tablecloth and then continue to add to it year after year. Or you can combine holiday decorating with expressions of thankfulness by making colored paper leaves, pumpkins and other holiday symbols for them to write on. Then use these paper symbols to dress your table. One way is to simply use pinking shear scissors to cut flannel fabric runners for your table. I like to use two different color fabrics cut at two different lengths and layer them. Then scatter the **HANDWRITTEN BLESSINGS** around a few candles, and you have a beautiful centerpiece. Sometime during the day take time to read the blessings to each other. Another idea is to tell stories from your past to each other. It reinforces the family bond.

INVITE SOMEONE WHO CANNOT CELEBRATE with his own family. An elderly person, a college student, or even a single friend from church or the community would welcome the opportunity and will be forever grateful. Make it a tradition. One family invited a new neighbor and sharing the holiday together became a tradition that lasted years.

MAKE THANKSGIVING LESS CHAOTIC. If you are hosting a Thanksgiving dinner, remember to try to keep balance in your life. Your home does not have to be immaculately clean or look like a show home. Don't strive for perfection in your cooking by choosing recipes that are too complicated. Decide with your mate on who will do what when it comes to straightening the house, planning, preparation, cooking and cleaning up responsibilities. In my family, everyone participates by contributing to the meal. Mom makes the turkey and the potatoes. Everyone else is designated by what he or she prefers to make: salad, vegetables, breads, desserts, etc. We all help clean up. And we all sit around and simply talk. It is perfectly wonderful.

CONSIDER HAVING YOUR OWN THANKSGIVING DAY dinner with only your immediate family. It is an ideal response for relieving stress and turmoil in your marriage if you find yourself struggling between choosing which family to spend the holiday with. You can join your families later for dessert.

> Lord, You are worthy of our praise and thanksgiving.
> You put food on our tables and love in our hearts.
> Let our praise and thanksgiving shine as a light
> to the world on the goodness of Your salvation. Amen.

Birthdays and Anniversaries

And in thee shall all families of the earth be blessed.

—GENESIS 12:3 (KJV)

Birthday parties date as far back as Bible times. We know this because there are two examples of birthdays being celebrated in the Bible. The first is in chapter forty of Genesis where we are told that the ruling Pharaoh celebrated his birthday by giving a great feast. It was during this party that Joseph's interpretations of dreams came true. The other birthday party in the Bible is fairly famous. In Mark chapter six, we read about King Herod's big feast to celebrate his own birthday.

Through much of history only well-known people such as saints, nobles, generals or national heroes celebrated birthdays. What I find interesting is the reason that birthday parties were held in the first place—it was feared that evil spirits were particularly attracted to people on their birthdays. To protect them from harm, friends and family gathered around to bring good thoughts and wishes. The well-wishers themselves were considered to be the best gift. It was only over time that the tradition evolved to the giving of birthday gifts.

In some countries, birthdays are not nearly as big a deal as they are here. Many children acquire baptismal or confirmational names from the saint associated with their date of birth, baptism or confirmation, and believing Eastern Orthodox Christians (and in some countries, Roman Catholics) mark the "name day" of the saint whose name they bear with special attention, often instead of birthday celebrations. In many parts of the world, individual birthdays go unnoticed. Instead, they have group birthday parties.

The first children's birthday parties occurred in Germany and were called Kinderfeste. They left the candles burning on the cake for the entire day. A member of the family would wake at sunrise and then light the candles. After dinner that night, everyone sang the birthday song and the birthday person blew out the candles. If all the candles were blown out in one try the wish would come true.

In Canada there is the tradition of greasing the nose of the birthday person with butter or margarine. The greased nose makes the child too slippery for bad luck to catch him.

In Denmark a flag is flown outside a window to designate that someone who lives there has a birthday. Presents are placed around the child's bed while he is sleeping so he will see them immediately upon awaking.

In Ecuador and Argentina, when a girl turns fifteen, there is a great celebration and she dances a waltz with her father.

In India, the birthday child wears a colored dress and passes out chocolates to the entire class, with the help of a trusted friend.

In Ireland and England, the child is lifted upside down and "bumped" on the floor for good luck. The number of bumps given is the age of the child plus one for good luck.

All of the traditions also have another important benefit. By celebrating milestones along the way to adulthood, we help strengthen our relationships with our children. Birthdays and anniversaries essentially represent the same thing: the number of years of living the person or couple has enjoyed. Nancy Twigg says, "Unlike Christmas and Valentine's Day, which fall on the same day for everyone who celebrates, birthdays and anniversaries are unique to the individual. These special occasions are like your own personal holidays that you can celebrate any way you wish. Birthdays reinforce the value of each individual, and they commemorate when the honoree became a part of the family unit and the value he brings to it. In the same way, anniversaries memorialize the sacred merging of two distinct lives into one new life together." We celebrate anniversaries to honor a couple's faithfulness to the commitment they made to each other.

LET'S DO IT AGAIN AND AGAIN

Traditions surrounding celebrations not only make the days unique, but are also a critical component of creating meaning and continuity in an ever-changing world. Guideposts writer Marilyn Morgan King discovered just how important traditions were to her family.

> There are six weeks during June and early July when we celebrate a family birthday every weekend. The parties are held at my house because it's the only one that's big enough for all fifteen of us to sit down together. Today it was Josh's special time.

We're nearing the end of the series, and I have to admit to some weariness. That's probably what brought on my impulsive suggestion that we have just one big party next year, celebrating them all at once. But I caught the shadow that passed across my son's face and quickly changed my mind. Life's not easy for Paul and Cheryl, with seven children and barely enough coming in each month to take care of necessities. Most of the time, they're all working very hard to make ends meet. There's not much time for frivolity and celebration.

Today we've laughed together, shared pizza, ice cream and birthday cake, and seventeen-year-old Josh has been reminded of how very special he is. The whole gang has gone to the school yard across the street now, except for two-year-old Joseph, who has curled up in Grandma's lap and fallen asleep. There's a wastebasket stuffed with gift wrap in the middle of the room; cake plates and licked-off candles on the table; helium balloons that have slipped out of small hands clinging to the ceiling; and lemonade glasses on all the end tables. But I know one sleepy boy and one tired grandma who can't think of a thing in the world they'd rather be doing.

The most celebratory thing you can do is to simply repeat what you have done before.

SIMPLICITY MADE SIMPLE

WRITE A BIRTHDAY BLESSING. There is nothing more sacred than life, and no words more precious than the Word of God. A birthday is the perfect occasion to use God's Word as a prayer blessing for someone's life. My favorite Scripture for such an occasion is Philippians 1:3–6. I particularly like the New Living Translation, which reads: "Every time I think of you, I give thanks to my God. I always pray for you, and I make my requests with a heart full of joy because you have been my partners in spreading the Good News about Christ from the time you first heard it until now. And I am sure that God, who began the good work within you, will continue his work until it is finally finished." You may even want to consider starting a new blessing tradition. Rather than presents, ask family members and guests to speak words of blessings that they wish for the birthday person during the coming year.

Take a trip down memory lane. Have family members tell about a specific memory they have of the birthday person or anniversary couple. Pull out the birthday person's baby book and read aloud. For the anniversary couple, use the guest list from their wedding as an invitation list for "special" anniversaries. Be sure to **ASK THE GUESTS TO BRING ALONG A SPECIAL MEMORY** of the couple as well.

Create lasting birthday memories. A simple way to do this is to give each family member a sheet, in similar fashion to the Thanksgiving tablecloth, to be used as the **BIRTHDAY TABLECLOTH**. Have guests sign it with permanent ink. Be sure to include the paw prints of the family's best friend too! After the party, parents can create a memory scrapbook of the party with photos and a few notes of things that happened at the party. Be sure to include a list of gifts as well.

HONOR WITH GIFTS TO CHARITY. Make it a tradition to give a gift to charity in honor of the birthday or anniversary. This could be in lieu of a gift. Let the honorees choose the charity.

PLANT A GIFT. When my goddaughter was little, her father planted a tree in her honor. Each year on her birthday, Dad measured the tree's diameter and my goddaughter's height to see which had grown the most over the past year. Planting a tree is also a wonderful anniversary gift. It easily symbolizes the growth in a marriage. Nancy Twigg says, "As the tree grows bigger and stronger, it will serve as a visual reminder that your relationship is also changing and growing each year."

SURPRISE THEM. Last year, several of my family individually called my answering machine while I was away and sang their unique version of "Happy Birthday." It was such a sweet surprise when I came home to listen to all of their voices—most of whom are several hundred miles away. Even my uncle in California joined in the chorus. I was thrilled. Elizabeth Berg, author of *Family Traditions*, has this wonderful suggestion for anyone who is going to be eighty or older: Contact the Greeting Office, The White House, Washington, DC 20500. Do this six weeks before the birthday arrives. They'll send a congratulatory message from the president.

Dear Lord, what I have learned about holidays
is that You ordained them to make us stop and remember
all that is good in our lives. I will not let another holy day
pass me by without celebrating the people and the
provisions that You have given me. Amen.

Conclusion

S t. Nicholas was a real person. He was the bishop of a church in Myra, a land of "green hills, warm sun and soft sea breezes" in the country now known as Turkey. Author Cristine Bolley wrote in her book, *A Gift from St. Nicholas*, that "St. Nicholas understood that life's real treasure is found in doing what is right in the eyes of God, and he discovered that joyful peace comes from loving others. He is remembered fondly for his anonymous efforts to give away his inherited wealth."

Now, all these hundreds of years later, our hearts are yearning for a Christmas past, like the one St. Nicholas knew. But the pace of our world today can make it seem as though it could never happen without a miracle. The good news is that we do have a miracle—we have been given the perfect gift for making the best Christmas ever—Christ. As we remember the simple birth of our Savior we can give thanks for the miracle of His life. But we can also offer hope with each gift we give for a renewal of His Spirit in the lives of those we love. Simply remind them of the blessing of the miracle, the hope and the wonder of Christ's life and death, and the impact it has had on our lives.

So rather than letting the sheer number of demands made on you during the holiday season hamper your spirit, find the joy that is hidden deep in your heart and share it with all those around you. Renew old friendships, revive family traditions and let the light of Bethlehem shine over you and all of your celebrations this year.

Notes

Part One—O Holy Night!

1. Melissa C. Stoppler, MD, "The Season to Be Tired," www.stressabout.com.

2. Christopher Hammon, "Handling Holiday Stress,"www.oates.org.

3. Morton C. Orman, MD, "A Special Report: How to Keep Stress and Tension from Ruining Your Holiday Season," www.stresscure.com.

4. Barbara H. Fiese et al., "A Review of Fifty Years of Research on Naturally Occurring Family Routines and Rituals: Cause for Celebration?" *Journal of Family Psychology* (2002): Volume 16, No. 4, 381–390.

5. Aaron Cobb, "Christmas—The Importance of Tradition," www.christianteens. about.com.

6. Ibid.

7. Juanita Thouin, "Holiday Traditions: More Important Than You May Think," www. mtsusidelines.com.

Part Two—'Tis the Season to Be Jolly

8. Adapted from Keith Varnum, "Survival Guide for the Holidays," www. theallineed.com.

9. "What Is Your Best Holiday Travel Tip?" *Real Simple Magazine* (December 2004), 51.

10. Joan C. Hawxhurst, *The Interfaith Family Guidebook* (Kalamazoo, Michigan: Dovetail Publishing, 1998), 53.

11. Ibid., 72.

12. "Coping with Depression and the Holidays," www.aagponline.org.

13. "Children and Depression During the Holidays," www.medicalmoment.org.

14. Ibid.

15. "Depression and the Holidays," www.medicalmoment.org.

16. "Rein in Rudeness—Start with the Holidays," www.wcpn.org.

17. "Rudeness on the Rise," www.forbes.com.

18. Ibid.

Part Three—Deck the Halls with Happiness

19. "Hang 'Em High (and Low)," *Real Simple Magazine* (December 2004), 282.

Part Four—The Perfect Gift

20. Nancy Loving Tubesing, EdD, and Donald A. Tubesing, MDiv, PhD, *Kicking Your Holiday Stress Habits* (Duluth, Minnesota: Pfeifer-Hamilton Publishers, 1996), 12.

21. Cynthia Yates, *The Complete Guide to Creative Gift-Giving* (Ann Arbor, Michigan: Servant Publications, 1997), 17.

22. "Time the Best Year 'Round Gift for the Elderly," www.montana.edu.

Part Five—Celebrating Life

23. Sarah Ban Breathnach, *Mrs. Sharp's Traditions—Reviving Victorian Family Celebrations of Comfort and Joy* (New York: Scribner/Simple Abundance Press, 1990), 77.